NEW GOLD EDITION

ENGLISH Firsthand ACCESS

Marc Helgesen

Steven Brown

John Wiltshier

Series Editor
Michael Rost

PEARSON
Longman

Published by
Pearson Longman Asia ELT
20/F Cornwall House
Taikoo Place
979 King's Road
Quarry Bay
Hong Kong

fax: +852 2856 9578
email: pearsonlongman.hk@pearson.com
www.pearsonlongman.com

and Associated Companies throughout the world.

© Pearson Education Asia Limited 2007

This book was developed for Longman Asia ELT by Lateral Communications Limited.

First edition 1990
Second edition 2000
This edition 2007
Reprinted 2008 (twice)

Produced by Pearson Education Asia Limited, Hong Kong
SWTC/04

PROJECT DIRECTOR, SERIES EDITOR: Michael Rost
PROJECT COORDINATOR: Keiko Kimura
PROJECT EDITOR: Allison Gray
ART DIRECTOR: Lisa Ekström
TEXT DESIGN: Lisa Ekström
PRODUCTION COORDINATOR: Rachel Wilson
AUDIO ENGINEER: Glenn Davidson
MUSIC: Music Bakery, Polarity Studios
WEBSITE COORDINATOR: Alan Medeiros
TESTING CONSULTANTS: Gary Buck, Natalie Chen
VOCABULARY CONSULTANT: Brett Reynolds
ILLUSTRATIONS: Terry Wong, Ryan Napoli, Norman Rainock,
Donna Turner, Lisa Ekström
PHOTOGRAPHS: Bananastock, Blue Moon, Brand X Pictures,
Dynamic Graphics, Iconotect, i dream stock, Image Source,
Image Zoo, Inmagine, MIXA, Photodisc, Pixtal, Rubberball,
Stockbyte, Tong Ro Image Photographers

ENGLISH FIRSTHAND ACCESS, NEW GOLD EDITION

Student Book with Self-Study CD
ISBN-13: 978-962-00-5813-4
ISBN-10: 962-00-5813-5

Teacher's Manual
ISBN-13: 978-962-00-5817-2
ISBN-10: 962-00-5817-8

CD-ROM Pack
ISBN-13: 978-962-00-5825-7
ISBN-10: 962-00-5825-9

Workbook
ISBN-13: 978-962-00-5815-8
ISBN-10: 962-00-5815-1

Classroom CD Pack Set
ISBN-13: 978-962-00-5819-6
ISBN-10: 962-00-5819-4

Introduction

Welcome to *English Firsthand Access!*

English Firsthand Access is the introductory level of the *English Firsthand New Gold* series. *English Firsthand Access* helps beginning students to communicate in English with confidence. We believe that:

- ***People learn English by <u>using</u> English.***
- ***With support, learners really can communicate in English, even from the beginning.***

For students to use English, they need:

- realistic language models
- personalized and motivating tasks
- language support (vocabulary, grammar and functional phrases)
- opportunities to communicate their own information, opinions and ideas.

The goal of *English Firsthand Access* is to meet those needs. The course provides activities for 40–50 hours of class work. Additional material in the *Teacher's Manual* provides for a total of 60 hours of class work.

Unit overview

Preview
Preview introduces a unified set of words that students will hear and use throughout the unit. Students listen to and say the words. Then they do a short activity with a partner to practice the words.

Listening
Listening makes use of the words the students have worked with in Preview and also introduces structures that learners will need for the Duet section.

- **Listen** is usually a more global listening. The students listen for main ideas and specific information.
- **Listen again** allows the students to hear the same audio program again. This time, however, they have a new task. Usually this task focuses on vocabulary or grammatical structures found in the unit.
- **About you** is a personalized task in which the speaker on the audio speaks directly to the learner.

Conversation
Conversation is a short dialog presented in a four-panel format. After practicing the given conversation, students make use of the "changes" presented under each picture. Finally, they use their own ideas to make similar conversations.

Duet

Pair work is the heart and soul of the *English Firsthand* series. In Duet, the students exchange information, opinions and ideas. This leads them to real communication, the goal of *English Firsthand Access*. Duet provides practical practice that is effective even in large classes, with personalized activities that build motivation. Simple, step-by-step instructions help students understand what to do.

- **Pronunciation** calls attention to target forms and gives guidance on stress and intonation, the most important aspect of improving pronunciation.
- **Think time** allows learners to preview the task and plan what they want to say.
- **Communication** is completed in pairs. It has a clear outcome that allows students to know they have succeeded.
- **Challenge** is an extension task for students who complete the main task.

Language Check

Language check allows students to consolidate grammar and vocabulary from the unit.

- **Grammar target** is a chart of the unit's grammar point.
- **Grammar check** is a short task that uses the target grammar.
- **Vocabulary check** reviews words from the unit.
- **Bonus** is additional communicative practice for students who complete the main tasks.

Language Check exercises are also available on-line at www.efcafe.com, along with self-correcting answer keys. If you choose to assign Language Check as homework, students may check it themselves at EFCafe and print it out to hand in. This provides students with immediate feedback and saves correction time.

Ensemble

Ensemble introduces functional language related to the unit.

- **Today's goal** makes it clear what the students must do.
- **Language models**: Students listen and complete a number of sentences. Students learn the new language as whole units.
- **Think time** allows students to plan what they will say.
- **Communication task**: The main task is done in groups.
- **How did I do?** asks students to evaluate their own learning.

Solo

Solo provides reading, listening and writing practice. It also introduces people from many different countries. Solo can be done as homework or in class. Solo activities are also available on-line at www.efcafe.com.

Other supporting features of *English Firsthand Access*

Unit Zero: Unit Zero is a warm-up lesson in which students introduce themselves and practice basic classroom language.

Review units: There is a short review unit after Units 6 and 12. Learners review and consolidate vocabulary, grammar and functions through pair work reviews, tasks and games.

 Extra Listening: Extra Listening in the back of the book provides additional listening practice for students to complete on their own. The Extra Listening section includes listening scripts with blanks to review key vocabulary and grammar patterns. Learners can use the Self-Study CD to fill in the blanks.

Vocabulary Maps: At the back of the book there is a Vocabulary Map for each unit that enables learners to review key vocabulary from the unit. The Vocabulary Map expands the vocabulary of the unit, to include other common lexical items. Common collocations are also given.

Teacher's Manual: The *Teacher's Manual* includes:
- complete lesson plans
- culture and language notes
- grammar and usage notes
- photocopiable expansion activities
- unit quizzes and tests

CD-ROM Pack contains:
- **Test Generator software**: The Test Generator allows teachers to construct their own unit tests and semester tests. The Test Generator contains a bank of items to generate quick tests to check Conversation, Grammar, Vocabulary, and Listening.
- **PowerPoint Teaching Tool**: The *English Firsthand* series PowerPoint Teaching Tool provides dynamic screen shots of parts of each unit to help teachers guide classroom activities.

Workbook: The *English Firsthand Access Workbook* provides systematic review of the Grammar and Vocabulary of each unit. The Workbook also offers reading comprehension exercises and additional listening practice, utilizing the Self-Study CD in the back of the Student Book.

The English Firsthand Café: The English Firsthand Café is a free website that offers online practice for students, discussion boards for teachers, and links to other learning resources for students and teachers. The EFCafé can be accessed directly at www.efcafe.com, or through the Companion Websites link at www.longman.com.

Your students will really be communicating and learning from each other. We hope they make a lot of progress–and have fun doing so. We also hope that you find teaching exciting and rewarding and that you and your learners continue to enjoy using English, firsthand.

> Good luck,
> Marc, Steve, John, the authors
> Michael and Allison, the editors
> Lisa and Keiko, the course designers

Contents

Contents

Acknowledgements

The authors would like to thank the many people who have used *English Firsthand Access* and who have offered ideas and suggestions for the series. We would also like to acknowledge some of our colleagues and teachers whose ideas we have incorporated into the books. In particular, we wish to thank:

Keith Adams
Charles Adamson
Soo Youn Ahn
Diana Ailenei
Daniel Allardyce
Kerry Allen
Ataya Aoki
Yoshimasa Awaji
Daralyn Bates
Elliott Brett
Andrew Chang
Nelson Chang
Doer Chen
Tina Chen
Yoon J. Choi
Doris Chueng
Heather Clemans
Anita Collins
Karen Cronin
Tony Crooks
Fidel Cruz

Chris Cuadra
Byron R. Davies
Stephen Dawe
Wesley DeJonge
Jack Eisner
John Fanselow
Ramon Fargus
Jesper Frederiksen
David Fournier
Evonne Fu
Cecilia Fujishima
Eva Gao
Judy Gilbert
Stephen Gordon
Peter Hamley
Sayaka Hayasaka
Brenda Hayashi
Bill Heffernan
Maiko Hikichi
Hsing Shu Hsiao
Jeff Huang

Yumiko Ito
Sang Soon Jeong
Jonathan Johnstone
Jae Hwan Jung
Tina Kennedy
Patrick Kiernan
Hyeon Hee Kim
Ivy Kim
Tae Kim
Yani Kim
Gerry Lassche
Eliza Liu
Alice Lee
Jessica Lee
Sung Yun Lee
Allison Lemke
Bill Lundergan
Curtis Mackenzie
Alan Maley
Philip McNally
Miho Moody

Simon Moran
Tim Murphey
Lee Gi Myung
Seiko Oguri
Sean O'Malley
Yumi Onodera
William Packard
Kwang-Il Park
Walter Park
Jackie Pels
Raymond Rose
Yuko Sakai
Ken Schmidt
Toyoko Schmidt
Eunice Shih
Katherine Song
Utako Sugano
Nancy Sun
Craig Sweet
Miki Takahashi
Masaki Takamatsu

Paul Tansey
Brian Tomlinson
Setsuko Toyama
Erik Turkelson
Charles Varcoe
Seo Jung Wah
Kent Wang
Scott Ward
Tom Warren-Price
Jim Wiltshier
Pat Wiltshier
Naoko Ouchi Witzel
Andrew Wright
Jocelyn Yang
Sandy Yang
Sarah Yin
Chie Yoshida

We would also like to thank our many friends and colleagues at Longman Asia ELT and in the various Pearson Education offices for their efforts in collecting information, talking to teachers, and sharing ideas. In particular, we wish to thank: Roy Gilbert, Rachel Wilson, Christienne Blodget, Tom Sweeney, Michael Chan, Keiko Sugiyama, Constance Mo, Moon-Jeong Lim;

the Japan team: Shinsuke Ohno, Minoru Ikari, Jonah Glick, Takashi Hata, Yuji Toshinaga, Steve King, Masaharu Nakata, Donn Ogawa, Yuko Tomimasu, Mari Hirukawa, Hiroko Nagashima, Megumi Takemura, Alastair Lamond, Michiyo Mitamura, Ken Sasaki, Takeshi Kamimura, Meiko Naruse, Tomoko Ayuse, Kenji Sakai, Reiko Murota, Mayumi Abe, Minako Uta, Masako Yanagawa, Ayako Tomekawa, Minoru Ikari, Katherine Mackay;

the Korea team: Yong Jin Oh, Chong Dae Chung, Jan Totty, Rilla Schram, Seung Hee Ji, Hyuk Jin Kwon, Tae Youp Kim, Sang Ho Bae;

the Taiwan team: Golden Hong, Louis Lin, Vivian Wang, Sherry Lin, Christine Huang, Joseph Chan, David Ger;

the Thailand team: Narerat Ancharepirat, Chris Allen, Unchalee Boonrakvanich, Udom Sathawara, Sura Suksingh.

We would also like to thank our editorial and design team for their countless ideas, insights and hard work: Michael Rost, Allison Gray, Lisa Ekström, and Keiko Kimura.

The authors contribute a portion of the royalties from the *English Firsthand* series to support girls' and basic education projects in the developing world through CARE. For more information, visit: www.care.org

This book is dedicated to our students, who made the project worthwhile, and to our families, Masumi and Kent Helgesen, Curt and Clara Brown, and Miyuki, George, and Hannah Wiltshier, for all their support.

Find someone who…

1   Read the questions.

2   Stand up. Ask the questions. Do they say "yes" or "no"?
Yes = write the name. No = ask a different question.
Use 1 name only 1 time.

Do you like	swimming?	Yes. I love it!
	dogs?	Yes. I love them.
		No, not really

   1 **Do you like** … chocolate ice cream?

I love it: _____
name

   6 … purple shirts?

I love them: _____

   **2** **Do you like** … dogs?

I love them: _____

   7 … swimming?

I love it: _____

   3 … karaoke?

I love it: _____

   8 … cats?

I love them: _____

   4 … long, hot baths?

I love them: _____

   9 … pizza?

I love it: _____

   5 … spicy food?

I love it: _____

   10 … roller coasters?

I love them: _____

3   Find a partner. Do you remember the names?
That's _____name_____. *She loves* _____.
That's _____name_____. *He loves* _____.

1 Learn classroom language. Look at the spaces.

2 💿 CD-1 **track 2** Listen. Write the missing words.

| did | excuse | ~~how~~ | pardon | sorry | what | what's |

1 ___How___ do you spell it?

2 ___what's___ does (that) mean?

3 ___what's___ (that) in English?

4 ___pardon___ ?

5 I'm ___sorry___ ?

6 ___excuse___ me?

Work with a partner. You are **A**. Use this page.
Your partner is **B**. **B**, use page 12.

1 **A**, ask these questions. Write **B**'s answers.

How do you spell it?

1 What's your name? _____ Ask:

2 What's your favorite food? _____

3 What's your favorite color? _____

4 What's your favorite sport? _____

5 What's your favorite TV show? _____

What's that in English?

Ask:

2 Listen to **B**. Ask these questions. Then answer **B**.

1 *Excuse me?*

2 *I'm sorry?*

3 *Pardon?*

4 *Excuse me?*

5 *I'm sorry?*

3 Close your books. Can you remember all 6 sentences from page 10? Write them.

Work with a partner. You are **B**. Use this page.
Your partner is **A**. **A**, use page 11.

1 Listen to **A**. Ask these questions. Then answer **A**.

1 *Pardon?*

2 *Excuse me?*

3 *I'm sorry?*

4 *Pardon?*

5 *I'm sorry?*

2 **B**, ask these questions. Write **A**'s answers.

How do you spell it?

1 What's your name? _____ Ask:

2 What's your favorite food? _____

3 What's your favorite color? _____

4 What's your favorite sport? _____

5 What's your favorite TV show? _____

What's that in English?

Ask:

3 Close your books. Can you remember all 6 sentences from page 10? Write them.

Ensemble *Interview your teacher*

GROUP TALK

1 → **TODAY'S GOAL:** Interview your teacher.

2 **Think Time** Plan your questions. Work alone or with a partner.
What do you want to ask? Write at least 3 questions.
You can use a dictionary.

1 _____

2 _____

3 _____

4 _____

IDEAS TO HELP YOU

- **Hometown:**
  Where are you from?

- **Interests:**
  *What do you do in
  your free time?*

- *What's your favorite
  _____?*

- *Do you like _____ ?*

- **Other:**
  *Do we have homework
  in this class?*

- *How can I learn English?*

3 **Action** Now ask questions. Write your teacher's answers.

13

Preview

1 CD-1 **track 3** Listen. Point to the pictures.

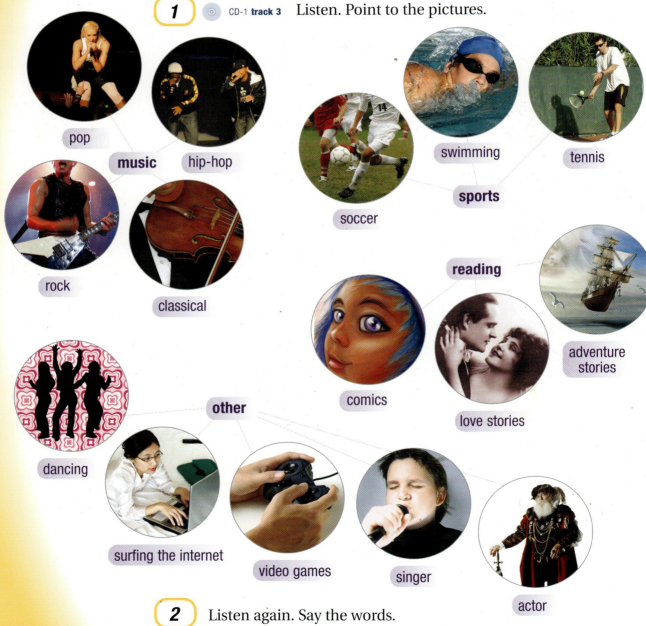

pop

music hip-hop

rock

classical

soccer

swimming

tennis

sports

reading

comics

love stories

adventure
stories

dancing

other

surfing the internet

video games

singer

actor

2 Listen again. Say the words.

3 Practice with a partner. Say the words. Partner, touch the
pictures quickly.

Listening *Tell me about yourself.*

1 ◎ CD-1 **tracks 4-6**   Listen. What do they say? Check (✓) your answers.

1 This is Kanjana.

- ☑ Bangkok
- ☐ sports
- ☑ pop

- ☐ Chiang Mai
- ☑ dancing
- ☐ classical

2 This is Eric.

- ☐ the US
- ☐ video games
- ☑ Diddy

- ☑ Canada
- ☑ surfing the internet
- ☐ 50 Cent

3 This is Ming.

- ☑ Taipei
- ☑ swimming
- ☐ adventure stories

- ☐ Hong Kong
- ☐ tennis
- ☑ love stories

2   Listen again. What "question words" do you hear? Check (✓) them.

1
- ☐ who
- ☑ what
- ☐ when
- ☑ where
- ☐ why
- ☐ what kind

2
- ☑ who
- ☑ what
- ☐ when
- ☑ where
- ☐ why
- ☐ what kind

3
- ☐ who
- ☑ what
- ☐ when
- ☑ where
- ☐ why
- ☐ what kind

About You   ◎ CD-1 **track 7**   Listen and answer.

1. _____

2. _____

3. _____

Compare answers with a partner.

1 CD-1 **track 8** Listen. Two students are at a party.

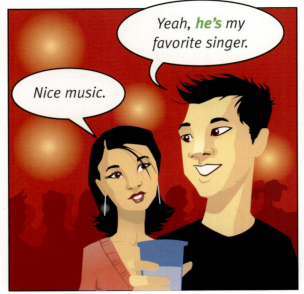

she's

Osaka Rio
Taipei New York

2 Practice with a partner. Use the **blue** and *green* words.

3 Make your own conversation. Use your ideas.

Duet A *Nice to meet you.*

Pronunciation   ◎ CD-1 **track 9**   Listen. Repeat silently. Then repeat out loud.

What	is	his	*last* name?	It's **West**.
Where	is	she	*from?*	**Bang**kok.
	are	you	*from?*	**Seoul**.
What	are	your	*int*erests?	I like **danc**ing.
	are	her	*interests?*	**She** likes to **read**.
Who	is	your	*fav*orite *act*or?	I like **John**ny **Depp**.

How do you spell it?

1   **Think Time**   Look at the information. Write information about yourself.

	First name	Last name	From	Favorite singer	Favorite actor	Interests
	Emma	Hart	London	Mariah Carey	Brad Pitt	dancing
	Jacob	W...				
	Sun Ae	Park	Busan	No one special	Leonardo DiCaprio	surfing the internet
	Chi-Ming					
You						
B						

2   You are **A**. Ask **B** about Jacob, Chi-Ming and **B**.

Do you like to exercise?

Sure.

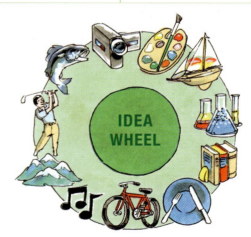

IDEA WHEEL

◗ **Challenge!**
Join another pair. Introduce **B**.
This is ... She's (he's) from ...

Pronunciation ◎ **CD-1 track 9** Listen. Repeat silently. Then repeat out loud.

What	*is*	*his*	**last** *name?*	*It's* **West**.
Where	*is*	*she*	**from**?	**Bang**kok.
	are	*you*	**from**?	**Seoul**.
What	*are*	*your*	**int**erests?	*I like* **danc**ing.
	are	*her*	**int**erests?	**She** likes to **read**.
Who	*is*	*your*	**fav**orite **act**or?	*I like* **John**ny **Depp**.

How do you spell it?

1 **Think Time** Look at the information. Write information about yourself.

	First name	Last name	From	Favorite singer	Favorite actor	Interests
	Emma	H...				
	Jacob	West	Melbourne	Destiny's Child	Johnny Depp	playing soccer
	Sun Ae					
	Chi-Ming	Lee	Shanghai	Usher	no one special	reading
You						
A						

2 You are **B**. Ask **A** about Emma, Sun Ae, and **A**.

*And do **you** like to exercise?*

I love it!

IDEA WHEEL

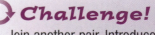
Challenge!
Join another pair. Introduce **A**.
This is ... She's (he's) from ...

Language Check

1 Grammar Target The verb "be." "Wh" and "yes / no" questions.

question word	+	(be)	+	subject	...?		subject	+	(be)	...
Where		are		you	from?		I		am	from Thailand.
Where		is		Hiro	from?		He		is	from Japan.
What		is		Hiro's last name	?		It		is	Tanaka.

(be)	+	subject	...?				
Are		Mana and Mali	from Thailand?	Yes,	they	are	from Bangkok.
Is		Naomi	from Tokyo?	No,	she	is	from Sapporo.

2 Grammar Check: Meeting new people

Write *am*, *is* or *are*. (8 points)

1 A: Where __are__ you from?

   B: I __am__ from Canada.

2 A: __is__ Marco from Spain?

   B: No, he __is__ from Mexico.

3 A: What __is__ Marco's last name?

   B: It __is__ Gonzales.

4 A: Where __are__ Sun Ae and An Jin from?

   B: They __are__ from Korea. Seoul _____ their hometown.

I am = I'm
He is = He's
She is = She's
It is = It's
You are = You're
They are = They're

3 Vocabulary Check: Free-time activities Write the verbs. (4 points)

surf	play	go	read	~~listen~~

A: Hey, Manee. Do you like music?

B: Sure. I _listen_ to rock music every day.

A: What about sports?

B: I __go__ swimming in my free time. How about you?

A: I __play__ soccer.

B: Do you like comic books?

A: Yeah! I __read__ comic books. I __surf__ the internet a lot, too.

B: Me, too. What's your email address?

Your score: _____ / 12

BONUS: Now practice the dialogue with a partner.

Ensemble *What do you like?*

MIXER

1 → **TODAY'S GOAL:** Interview 4 or more people

2 **Language Models** ⊙ CD-1 **track 10** Listen and complete.

Hi. How's *i t* _g o_ _ _ _ ? I'm John.

_N_ _ _ _ to _m_ _ _ _ you.

_C_ an _ interview _y_ _ _ , please?

_ _ you like sports?

_Wh_ _ _ type of sports?

_ _ you like _l_ _ _ _ _ _ _ _ _ to _m_ _ _ _ _ ?

_C l_ _ _ _ _ _ _ ? Rock?

Excuse me?

3 **Think Time** Plan your interview. Write questions.

1 _____

2 _____

3 _____

4 _____

IDEAS TO HELP YOU
- **computer games**
- **the internet / sites**
- **movies**
- **reading / books**
- **boys!**
- **girls!**
- **coffee shops**
- (your idea) _____

4 **Action** Stand up. Move. Interview someone.
Check a box. ☑
Then, do it again.

Remember **TODAY'S GOAL!**

☐ 1st interview

☐ 2nd interview

☐ 3rd interview

☐ 4th interview

Even more interviews? ☐ ☐ ☐

You can do it!

5 **How did I do?**
- ☐ I did very well.
- ☐ I did well.
- ☐ I did OK.
- ☐ I had trouble.
- ☐ I had BIG trouble!

Now fill in the chart on page 121.

Solo *Nice to meet you!*

1 Read about Chung Min, Jose, and Kate. Fill in the blanks. There are two extra words.

| mother | high | ~~name~~ | playing | from | great | business | bad |

This is Chung Min.

My __name__ is Chung Min. I'm from Korea. I'm studying _____ at the University of Queensland in Australia.

This is Jose.

Hi, I'm Jose. I'm from Mexico. I'm a _____ school student. I like _____ soccer.

This is Kate.

I'm Kate. I'm _____ Dublin. I teach in Taiwan. My students are _____!

2 CD-1 **tracks 11-13** Now listen. Check your answers.

3 *My writing:* Write about **yourself**.

 *Good job!*

On Your Own

- Extra Listening, page 122. Self-Study CD, tracks 3-5.
- Conversation. Listen and repeat. Self-Study CD, track 6.
- Solo. Listen and read. Self-Study CD, track 7.
- Language Check, Solo, Extra Practice www.efcafe.com.

21

unit 2   Write your name.

 **Preview**

1 ⊚ CD-1 **track 14** Listen. Point to the pictures.

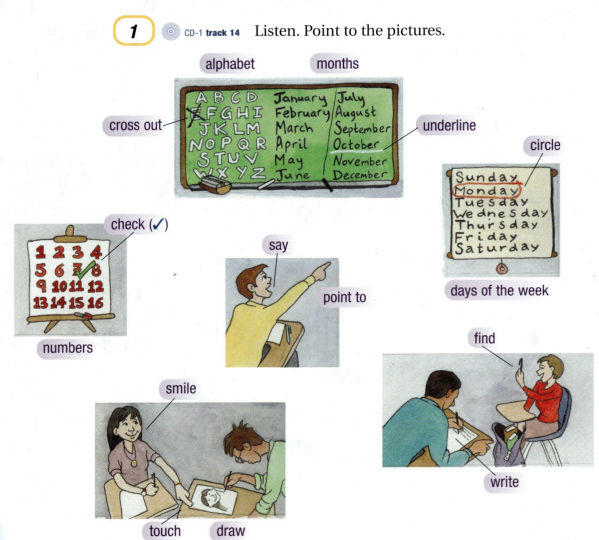

alphabet   months

cross out

underline

circle

check (✓)

say

point to

days of the week

numbers

find

smile

write

touch   draw

2 Listen again. Say the words.

3 Practice with a partner. A: point to "Wednesday."
B: Touch "September."

Listening *Do this. Pardon?*

1 CD-1 **tracks 15-20** Follow the instructions.

2 Listen again. Write the first word you hear. Which question do you hear? Check (✓) it.

1 *Write*   ☑ *Pardon?*   ☐ *I'm sorry?*

2 Francisco   ☐ *I'm sorry?*   ☑ *Excuse me?*

3 check   ☐ *Pardon?*   ☐ *Did you say B or V?*

4 circle   ☐ *I'm sorry?*   ☐ *Did you say 16 or 60?*

5 Draw   ☐ *Excuse me?*   ☑ *What does that mean?*

6 write   ☐ *Pardon?*   ☑ *How do you spell it?*

About You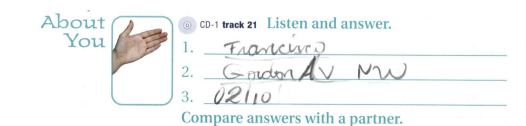

CD-1 **track 21** Listen and answer.

1. Francisco
2. Gordon Av NW
3. 02/10

Compare answers with a partner.

1 CD-1 **track 22** Listen. A foreign student is at an international airport.

Fill out this card, please.

OK.

Right.
I see.   hometown
address

What does **destination** *mean?*

It means **"the place you are going."**

the place you are from
the place you live

Oh, write your **name** *here.*

I see.

address
hometown   *Thank you.*

Now take it over there.

Thanks.

OK.
Right.

2 Practice with a partner. Use the **blue** and **green** words.

3 Make your own conversation. Use your ideas.

Duet A *Do you understand?*

Pronunciation ◎ CD-1 **track 23**   Listen. Repeat silently. Then repeat out loud.

Find box **number 8**.	*OK*.
Write your **name**. Do you under**stand**?	**Yes. Fine.**
What's your **phone num**ber?	607-555-2971
Your turn.	*OK*. **Find** box **14**.

Did you say B or V?

1 **Think Time** Look at the **blue** tasks. Do you understand them?

1	2	3	4	5	6
Write your name. Now spell your name. I'll write it. _____	☑ 13 ☑ 30	Say your hometown. Write it. I'll write it, too. _____	*Francisco*	What's your phone number? Say it. I'll write it, too. _____	*319-346.4538*
7	**8**	**9**	**10**	**11**	**12**
Check "50." ☐ 15 ☐ 50	*February 10*	Write these letters: B F H V P		When is your birthday? Say it. I'll write it, too. _____	⟨19⟩ 90
13	**14**	**15**	**16**	**17**	**18**
Draw a tree.	*miches*	Circle "17." 17 70	*L,t,r,D,w*	Smile. Now check "OK." ☐ right ☐ OK	☑ right ☐ OK

2 Read the **blue** tasks. **B** will do them. Answer **B**'s questions.
Read the tasks in any order (1 - 17 - 9 - 3, etc.).
Do what **B** says. When you don't understand, ASK.

3 Look at **B**'s page. Is it the same as yours?

Challenge!
Close your book. You added 8 things. B added 8 things. Can you remember all 16?

25

Duet B *Do you understand?*

Pronunciation ⊙ CD-1 **track 23** Listen. Repeat silently. Then repeat out loud.

Find box **num**ber **8**.	**O**K.
Write your **name**. Do you under**stand**?	**Yes**. **Fine**.
What's your **phone num**ber?	607-555-2971
Your turn.	**O**K. **Find** box **14**.

Did you say B or V?

1 **Think Time** Look at the **green** tasks. Do you understand them?

1	2 Check "13." ☐ 13 ☐ 30	3	4 Write your name. Now spell your name. I'll write it.	5	6 What's your phone number? Write it. I'll write it, too.
7 ☐ 15 ☐ 50	8 When is your birthday? Write it. I'll write it, too.	9	10 Draw a car.	11	12 Circle "19." 19 90
13	14 Say your hometown. Write it. I'll write it, too.	15 17 70	16 Write these letters: L T R D W	17 ☐ right ☐ OK	18 Smile. Check "right." ☐ right ☐ OK

2 Read the **green** tasks. **A** will do them. Answer **A**'s questions.
Read the tasks in any order (4 - 16 - 8 - 10, etc.).
Do what **A** says. When you don't understand, ASK.

3 Look at **A**'s page. Is it the same as yours?

↻ Challenge!
Close your book. You added 8 things. A added 8 things. Can you remember all 16?

 # Language Check

1 Grammar Target: Imperatives: Orders and instructions

Positive		Negative		
verb		*don't*	+	**verb**
Write	your name here.	*Don't*	**write**	your phone number.
Circle	your name.	*Don't*	**underline**	it.

don't = do not

2 Grammar Check: *Filling out a form*

You are Jill Jackson. Look at the picture. Write positive and negative sentences. Use *circle*, *underline*, *write* and *check*. (6 points)

1   _Write your name_____ on line one.
    Don't write your name on line two.

2   ___Don't Creck___ the "teacher" box.
    ___Check h___ the "student" box.

3   ___circle___ "female."
    ___Don't circle___ "male."   Circule
    Don't

4   ___underin___ your last name.
    ___Don't underin___ your first name.

> on the lines below.
> 1. *Jill Jackson*
>   (name)
> 2. _____
>   (address)
>
> ☐ teacher   ☑ student
>
> (female) / male
>
> Jill Jackson

3 Vocabulary Check: *Numbers, days, months*

Write the missing numbers, days, and months. (6 points)

1 _one_ two _three_ four five six seven _eight_ nine ten

2 Sunday _monday_ Tuesday Wednesday _thurday_ Friday Saturday

3 January _February_ March April May June July August
   September _october_ November December

Your score: _____ / 12

BONUS: Give your partner 5 instructions. "Circle April." "Check Monday." "Underline one."

Ensemble *Do this.*

MIXER

1 → **TODAY'S GOAL: Talk with 4 or more people**

APRIL

Mon.	Tue.	Wed.	Thu.	Fri.	Sat.	Sun.
	1	2	3	4	5	6
7	8	9	10 *today* ✱	11	12	13
14	15	16	17	18	19	20
21	22	23	24	25	26	27
28	29	30				

2 **Language Models** ◎ CD-1 **track 24** Listen and complete. Today is **April 10.**

Circle A _ _ _ _ _ 28th.

C _ _ _ _ _ out yesterday.

C _ _ _ _ _ _ your favorite day of the week.

Write your n _ _ _ at the top of the calendar.

Check next _ _ _ _ _ day.

D _ _ _ _ a flower on April 23rd.

Underline A _ _ _ _ _ 1st.

IDEAS TO HELP YOU

- **today**
- **tomorrow**
- **yesterday**
- **your birthday**
- **next Sunday**
- **last Friday**

3 **Think Time** Write five instructions.

1 _____

2 _____

3 _____

4 _____

5 _____

4 **Action** Find a partner.
Read your instructions.
Partner, follow them.
Check a box for each partner. ✔
Then change partners.

Remember **TODAY'S GOAL!**

☐ 1st person

☐ 2nd person

☐ 3rd person

☐ 4th person

You did it!

Pardon?

5 **How did I do?**

☐ I did very well.

☐ I did well.

☐ I did OK.

☐ I had trouble.

☐ I had BIG trouble!

Now fill in the progress chart on page 121.

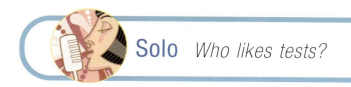
1 Read about Fatih and Mei. Fill in the blanks. There are two extra words.

~~good~~   enjoy   bad   cute   ideas   sleep   luck   one   four

This is Fatih from Turkey.

I'm a __good__ student, but I hate tests. Here are
my _____ for test taking:

1. read your class notes
2. get a good night's _____ before the test
3. relax
4. get a good _____ charm. I bring my lucky frog!

This is Mei from Taiwan.

I like tests. I _____ the challenge. I like his
idea number _____. I have a lucky cat. My
lucky cat's name is Samantha. She's lucky and
she's _____, too!

2 CD-1 **tracks 25-26** Now listen. Check your answers.

3 **My writing:** Do **you** like tests? Do you have a lucky charm? Think about it. Write about it.

Have some fun with
your new words!

On Your Own

- Extra Listening, page 122. Self-Study CD, tracks 8-13.
- Conversation. Listen and repeat. Self-Study CD, track 14.
- Solo. Listen and read. Self-Study CD, track 15.
- Language Check, Solo, Extra Practice www.efcafe.com.

Preview

1 CD-1 **track 27** Listen. Point to the pictures.

on your desk

pencils

eraser

pen

paper

notebook

folders

ruler

dictionary

in your room

desk

chair

lamp

computer

laptop

printer

in your backpack

MP3 player

camera

in your bag

wallet

sunglasses

lipstick

snacks

gum

bottled water

2 Listen again. Say the words.

3 Practice with a partner.
Close your book. How many words can you remember?

There is a pen. There is an eraser.
There are two pencils.

Listening *What's in your bag?*

1 ◎ CD-1 **tracks 28-31**   People are describing what's in their bags. Listen.
Circle the items they describe.

1

2

3

4

2 Listen again. Circle true or false.

1 He likes listening to music.   (T)   F

2 This is her sports bag.   T   F

3 It's a sunny day.   T   F

4 She reads on the train.   T   F

About You

◎ CD-1 **track 32**   Listen and answer.

1. _____

2. _____

3. _____

Compare answers with a partner.

31

Conversation *Excuse me?*

1 CD-1 **track 33**   Listen. A student is shopping at an office store.

Excuse me.

Yes.

Pardon me.

I need **an office chair.**

The **chairs** are over there. Next to the wall.

a computer
a desk

computers
desks

Thanks. And I need **a lamp.**

Lamps? Over here next to the window.

bookshelf

Shelves?

No problem.

Great. Thanks.

Sure.

2   Practice with a partner. Use the **blue** and **green** words.

3   Make your own conversation. Use your ideas.

Duet A   *What's on your desk?*

Pronunciation   ⊙ CD-1 **track 34**   Listen. Repeat silently. Then repeat out loud.

Is	there	a com**pu**ter?	**Yes**, there's **one** on the **desk**.
			No, no com**pu**ters.
Is	there	an e**ras**er?	**Yes**, it's on the **tab**le.
			Yes, there are **two**.

Excuse me?

1   **Think Time**   Look at page 30. Choose eight things. Write or draw them on your page.

☐ dictionary   ☐ eraser   ☐ notebook   ☐ ruler   ☐ pencil
☐ folder   ☐ printer   ☐ camera   ☐ laptop

2   Ask about **B**'s picture. Add **B**'s things to your picture.

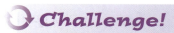

✐ Challenge!
Close your book.
You added 8 things. **B** added 8 things.
Can you remember all 16?

Pronunciation ⊚ CD-1 **track 34** Listen. Repeat silently. Then repeat out loud.

Is	there	a comp**u**ter?	**Yes,** there's **one** on the **desk**.
			No, no comp**u**ters.
Is	there	an e**ras**er?	**Yes,** it's on the **tab**le.
			Yes, there are **two**.

Excuse me?

1 **Think Time** Look at page 30. Choose eight things. Write or draw them on your page.

☐ dictionary ☐ eraser ☐ notebook ☐ ruler ☐ pencil
☐ folder ☐ printer ☐ camera ☐ laptop

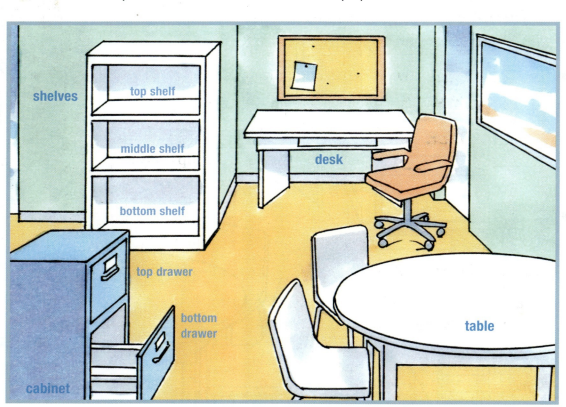

2 Ask about **A**'s picture. Add **A**'s things to your picture.

⟲ Challenge!
Close your book.
You added 8 things. **A** added 8
things. Can you remember all 16?

Language Check

1 **Grammar Target:** *There is / There are*

there is	+	singular nouns	
There is		**a computer**	on the desk.
There is		**an office chair**	in my office.
there are	+	plural nouns	
There are		**two computers**	on the desk.
There are		**two office chairs**	in my office.

a or an?
a + consonant (b, c, d, f, g...)
an + vowel (a, e, i, o, u)

2 **Grammar Check:** *In the office* Write *There is* or *There are*. (7 points)

1 *There are* four books on the top shelf.

2 _____ a laptop in his bag.

3 _____ an MP3 player on the desk.

4 _____ ten folders in the filing cabinet.

5 _____ a lamp on the green filing cabinet.

6 _____ three pens and a pencil in the top drawer.

7 _____ a notebook on the filing cabinet.

8 _____ three posters on the wall.

3 **Vocabulary Check:** *Personal items* Write the name of the item. (5 points)

camera	ruler	sunglasses	laptop	~~notebook~~
wallet	lipstick	pencil	MP3 player	pen

1 You write in this in English class: _____*notebook*_____ .

2 You put your money in this: _____ .

3 You take photographs with this: _____ .

4 You use the internet with this: _____ .

5 You listen to music with this: _____ .

6 You wear these on sunny days: _____ .

Your score: _____ / 12

BONUS: Make definitions for the other words. Partner, guess the word.

35

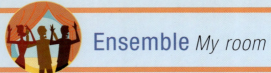

Ensemble *My room*

LINE-UP

1 → **TODAY'S GOAL:** "Shadow" with 3 people
Shadow = Listen and repeat.
(1st person for 90 seconds, 2nd for 75 seconds, 3rd for 60 seconds)

2 **Language Models** 💿 CD-1 **track 35** Listen and complete.

My room is _ _ _.

My room faces *s* _ _ _ _ _.

There are two *w* _ _ _ _ _ _ _, so my room is *w* _ _ _ and *br* _ _ _ _ _.

I like the *p* _ _ _ _ _ _ _ in my room.

I _ _ _ _ _ my room!

How about _ _ _ ?

How do you spell that?

IDEAS TO HELP YOU

- **warm / cold**
- **bright / dark**
- **curtains**
- **floor**
- **posters**
- **photos**
- **colors**
- **small / big**

3 **Think Time** Plan how to talk about your room. Make notes.

1 _____

2 _____

3 _____

4 _____

4 **Action** Stand up. Make 2 lines.
Face your partner.
Talk about your room.
Shadow your partner.

Remember **TODAY'S GOAL!**
Your teacher will check the time.

My room is small.
My room is small.
SHADOW SHADOW SHADOW

Change partners like this:

● ● ● ● ● ●
● → ● → ● → ● → ● → ●
← ← ← ← ← ← ←

5

How did I do?

	90	75	60
I did very well.	☐	☐	☐
I did well.	☐	☐	☐
I did OK.	☐	☐	☐
I had trouble.	☐	☐	☐
I had BIG trouble!	☐	☐	☐

Now fill in the progress chart on page 121.

1 Read about Chie and Mary. Fill in the blanks. There are two extra words.

an ~~busy~~ bookshelf sometimes before wooden after clean time last

This is Chie from Japan.

This is my English teacher's room. My teacher is very
___busy___ so his room is very messy. In Japan we get
earthquakes _____ . Maybe there was
_____ earthquake and he didn't have _____
to clean up.

This is Mary from New York.

My room is very neat and _____ . It's
very simple. My room has white walls and a
_____ floor. I keep my books, magazines
and photographs on my _____ . Do
you like my chair? I got it _____ week in a
sale. It's really comfortable!

2   CD-1 **tracks 36-37**   Now listen. Check your answers.

3 **My writing:** Is **your** room clean? What is
in your room? Think about your room.
Write about it.

Point around your room and practice
your new English words.

On Your Own

- Extra Listening, page 123. Self-Study CD, tracks 16-19.
- Conversation. Listen and repeat. Self-Study CD, track 20.
- Solo. Listen and read. Self-Study CD, track 21.
- Language Check, Solo, Extra Practice www.efcafe.com.

Preview

1   ◎ CD-1 **track 38**   Listen. Point to the pictures.

2   Listen again. Say the words and phrases.

3   Practice with a partner.

I get up at 7 a.m.   *Me, too.*
                         I don't. I get up at 7:30.

1 CD-1 **tracks 39-44**   People are talking about things they do every day. Listen. What are they talking about? Number the pictures, 1-6. There is one extra.

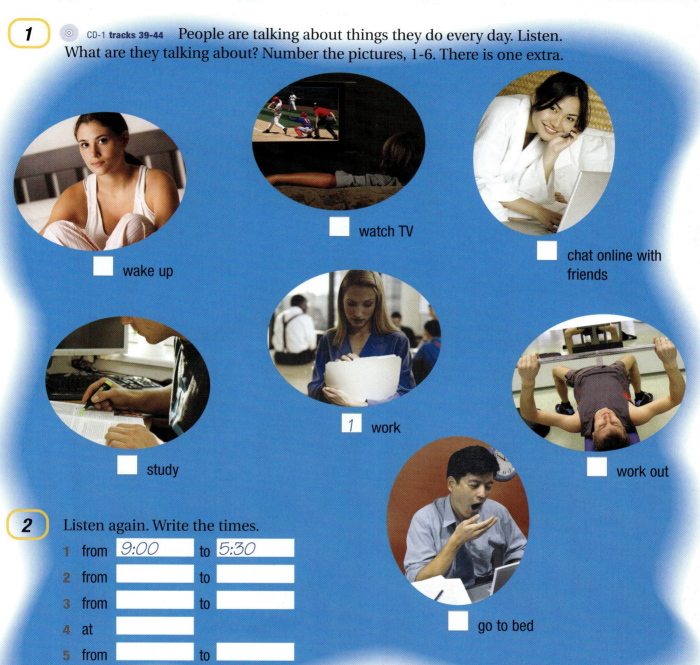

☐ watch TV

☐ wake up

☐ chat online with friends

☐ study

1 work

☐ work out

☐ go to bed

2 Listen again. Write the times.

1 from *9:00* to *5:30*
2 from ☐ to ☐
3 from ☐ to ☐
4 at ☐
5 from ☐ to ☐
6 at ☐

About You   CD-1 **track 45** Listen and answer.

1. _____
2. _____
3. _____

Compare answers with a partner.

1 CD-1 **track 46** Listen. Two friends are sitting in a coffee shop.

What time is it?

Um. It's ten **after** five.

to class

Oh no! I start **work** at 5:00.

Oops! You're late.

Oh no!

Do you have any money?

Go! I'll pay.

Hurry!

Thanks!

No problem.

Good luck. *You're welcome.*

2 Practice with a partner. Use the **blue** and **green** words.

3 Make your own conversation. Use your ideas.

Pronunciation   CD-1 **track 47**   Listen. Repeat silently. Then repeat out loud.

Do	you	eat **break**fast	every **day**?	**Yes**, I **do**.
				No, I **don't**.
Does	**she**	study	on **Sa**turday?	**Yes**, she **does**.
	he	work **out**		**No**, he **does**n't.
When	do	**you**	eat **break**fast?	At **sev**en o'**clock**.
	does	**she**	**stu**dy?	From **three** to **five**.

...eat lunch? — Yes, I do!

1 **Think Time** Look at the questions. Circle yes or no. Write the times.

Do you...	Yes	No	When do you...
... eat breakfast every day?	Yes	No	_____
... chat with friends every day?	Yes	No	_____
... eat a big dinner on Sunday?	Yes	No	_____

Did you say 6:15 or 6:50?

2 You are **A**. Ask about Erika.

Does Erika...	Yes	No	When does she...
... get up early every day?	Yes	No	_____
... watch TV every night?	(Yes)	No	*from 9 to 10:30*
... do homework every night?	Yes	No	_____

3 You are **A**. Ask about David.

Does David...	Yes	No	When does he...
... take the train or bus every day?	(Yes)	No	*at 8:00*
... work out every day?	Yes	No	_____
... study every night?	Yes	(No)	*not on Friday or Saturday*

4 Ask about **B**.

Does B...	Yes	No	When does B...
... go to bed late every night?	Yes	No	_____
... eat lunch every day?	Yes	No	_____
... study on Sunday night?	Yes	No	_____

Challenge!
Close your book.
How much can you
remember about **B**?

Duet B *When do you do that?*

  CD-1 **track 47** Listen. Repeat silently. Then repeat out loud.

Do	you	eat **break**fast	every **day**?	**Yes**, I **do**.
				No, I **don't**.
Does	**she**	study	on **Sat**urday?	**Yes**, she **does**.
	he	work **out**		**No**, he **doesn't**.
When	do	**you**	eat **break**fast?	At **se**ven o'**clock**.
	does	**she**	**stud**y?	From **three** to **five**.

…eat lunch? — Yes, I do!

---

1 (**Think Time**) Look at the questions. Circle yes or no. Write the times.

Do you…	Yes	No	When do you…
… eat breakfast every day?	Yes	No	_____
… chat with friends every day?	Yes	No	_____
… eat a big dinner on Sunday?	Yes	No	_____

Did you say 6:15 or 6:50?

2 You are **B**. Ask about Erika.

Does Erika…	Yes	No	When does she…
… get up early every day?	(Yes)	No	*at 7:00*
… watch TV every night?	Yes	No	_____
… do homework every night?	Yes	(No)	*not on Friday or Saturday*

3 You are **B**. Ask about David.

Does David…	Yes	No	When does he…
… take the train or bus every day?	Yes	No	_____
… work out every day?	(Yes)	No	*from 2 to 3:30*
… study every night?	Yes	No	_____

4 Ask about **A**.

Does A…	Yes	No	When does A…
… go to bed late every night?	Yes	No	_____
… eat lunch every day?	Yes	No	_____
… study on Sunday night?	Yes	No	_____

Challenge!
Close your book.
How much can you
remember about **A**?

Language Check

1 **Grammar Target:** *Do / Does: yes / no questions and short answers*

Yes / No questions					Short answers		
do / does +	subject	+	verb	…?		subject +	**do / does**
Do	you		*take*	the train every day?	Yes,	I	**do.**
Do	Rick and Erika		*watch*	TV every night?	No,	they	**don't.**
Does	David		*study*	every night?	Yes,	he	**does.**
Does	Chie		*wake up*	early every morning?	No,	she	**doesn't.**

2 **Grammar Check:** *Schedules*   Unscramble the questions. (5 points)

1 every you out do work day ?   *Do you work out every day?*_____ .

2 Rick early up morning every does get ? _____ .

3 eat morning do every breakfast they ? _____ .

4 bed night go you late do every to ? _____ .

5 night Erika watch does TV every ? _____ .

6 the take every David day does bus ? _____ .

3 **Vocabulary Check:** *Everyday actions*   Write the phrases under the pictures. Use the phrases from the box. There is one extra phrase. (7 points)

work out	~~eat dinner~~	chat on-line	get up	finish class
study	take the bus	start work	go to bed	

1 *eat dinner*____   2 _____   3 _____   4 _____

5 _____   6 _____   7 _____   8 _____

Your score: _____ / 12

BONUS: Work with a partner. Look on page 38. Find: *get up, go to bed, finish class, work out, eat dinner*

Ensemble *When is it?*

GROUP TALK

1 → **TODAY'S GOAL:** Ask 3 questions to ALL your group.

2 **Language Models** CD-1 **track 48** Listen and complete.

OK, my first q _ _ _ _ _ _ _ _ .

When is your f _ _ _ _ _ _ _ _ time of day?

L _ _ _ _ _ time!

How about _ _ _, Tom?

And Miki?

N _ _ _ question. What time don't you like? Why not?

What do you do in the evening?

I'm sorry?

3 **Think Time** Plan your questions. Make notes.

1 _____

2 _____

3 _____

IDEAS TO HELP YOU
- dinner time
- time at home
- night time
- bed time
- coffee time
- in the evening
- in the morning
- in the afternoon

4 **Action** Make a group of 3–4.
Ask your questions.
Listen to the answers.
React to the answers: *Great! Why? Why not?*
No way! Really! Are you sure?

Remember **TODAY'S GOAL!**

5 **How did I do?**
☐ I did very well.
☐ I did well.
☐ I did OK.
☐ I had trouble.
☐ I had BIG trouble!
Now fill in the progress chart on page 121.

Solo *Is 7:30 a.m. early?*

1 Read about Myong Hee, Rick, and Pepper. Fill in the blanks. There are two extra words.

~~high~~	late	early	south	grandmother
very	bed	eight	nice	student

This is Myong Hee from Korea.

*I'm a high school student. I get up _____ .
I get up at six. I have no time for breakfast. My
mother gets up early and my _____
gets up very early.*

This is Rick from New Zealand.

*I'm a _____ at university. I get
up _____. I get up at seven
thirty. I eat a big breakfast with my dog.*

This is Pepper. She's Rick's dog.

*I get up _____ early at about 4. I eat
breakfast with Rick at _____. Rick goes to
university at nine and I go back to _____ !*

2 ⊙ CD-1 **tracks 49-51** Now listen. Check your answers.

On Your Own

- Extra Listening, page 123. Self-Study CD, tracks 22-27.
- Conversation. Listen and repeat. Self-Study CD, track 28.
- Solo. Listen and read. Self-Study CD, track 29.
- Language Check, Solo, Extra Practice www.efcafe.com.

3 **My writing:** What time do **you** get up?
Is it early like Rick?
Write about it.

 What time do you go to bed?

45

Preview

1   ⊙ CD-1 **track 52**   Listen. Point to the pictures.

2   Listen again. Say the words.

3   Practice with a partner.

Is your father quiet?   *Yeah. Pretty quiet.*

Is your dad lazy?   *Lazy? Not really. He's hardworking.*

Listening *Tell me about your family.*

1 ◎ CD-1 **tracks 53-55** Listen. Which words do you hear? Check (✔) the boxes.

1
- ☐ hardworking
- ☐ happy
- ✔ serious
- ☐ shy
- ☐ friendly
- ☐ outgoing

2
- ☐ happy
- ☐ healthy
- ☐ pretty
- ☐ nice
- ☐ smart
- ☐ quiet

3
- ☐ funny
- ☐ shy
- ☐ quiet
- ☐ friendly
- ☐ serious
- ☐ lazy

2 Listen again. Write the words from step 1 next to the people.

1 mother _____
father *serious*
sister _____
brother _____

2 mother _____
father _____
grandmother _____
sister _____

3 mother _____
father _____
cat _____
dog _____

About You ◎ CD-1 **track 56** Listen and answer.

1. _____
2. _____
3. _____

Compare answers with a partner.

1 CD-1 **track 57** Listen. Two friends are walking down the street.

Who's that?

My **sister**.

brother *his*

Really? Is that **her** motorcycle?

Yeah.

Do you like it?

It's great.

What does **she** do?

She's a musician.

he *He's*

So what's **she** like?

She's really **shy**.

he *He's* *quiet* *funny*

2 Practice with a partner. Use the **blue** and **green** words.

3 Make your own conversation. Use your ideas.

Duet A *My family*

Pronunciation   ◎ CD-1 **track 58**   Listen. Repeat silently. Then repeat out loud.

Who's **this**?	**That's** my **mom**.
What does she **do**?	She **works** in an **office**.
What's she **like**?	She's **ver**y hard**work**ing.
What does she **like** to **do**?	She likes **dan**cing.
Tell me about your **pet**.	I don't **have** one.

What's (that) in English?

---

1   **Think Time**   Draw a simple picture of your family.
Think of three sentences to say about each person.

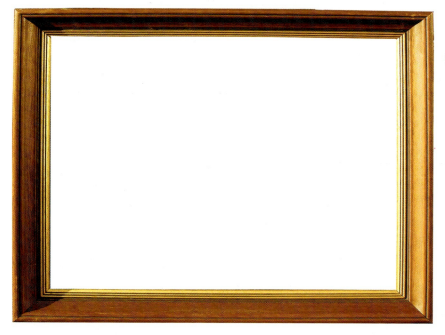

*Hint:
Simple pictures
are best!*

---

2   Show your picture to **B**.
Tell **B** about each person.
B, ask a question about each person.

3   Look at **B**'s picture. Ask a question about each person.

4   Look at **B**'s picture again. How much can you remember?

Challenge!
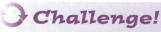
Change partners. Tell a new partner
about your family.

Pronunciation ◎ CD-1 **track 58** Listen. Repeat silently. Then repeat out loud.

Who's **this**?	**That's** my **mom**.
What does she **do**?	She **works** in an **off**ice.
What's she **like**?	She's **very** hard**work**ing.
What does she **like** to **do**?	She likes **dan**cing.
Tell me about your **pet**.	I don't **have** one.

What's (that) in English?

1 (**Think Time**) Draw a simple picture of your family.
Think of three sentences to say about each person.

Hint:
Simple pictures
are best!

2 Look at **A**'s picture. Ask a question about each person.

3 Show your picture to **A**.
Tell **A** about each person.
A, ask a question about each person.

4 Look at **A**'s picture again. How much can you remember?

↻ **Challenge!**
Change partners. Tell a new partner
about your family.

Language Check

1 Grammar Target: Wh- questions

question word	+	do / does	+	subject	+	verb?	
What		**do**		you		**do?**	
What		**do**		your mom and dad		**like to do?**	
What		**does**		your sister		**do?**	
What		**does**		your brother		**like to do?**	

question word	+	(be)	+	subject	+	?	
Who		**is**		this?			
What		**is**		your sister		like?	
Who		**are**		they?			
What		**are**		your brothers		like?	

2 Grammar Check: Talking about family   Write a question for the answers.   (5 points)

1   *What is your brother like?*
My brother is funny and outgoing.

2   _____
That is my mom.

3   _____
My sister works in an office.

4   _____
I am a musician.

5   _____
My mom and dad like to play tennis.

6   _____
My dog is friendly!

3 Vocabulary Check: Personality opposites   Write the words.   (7 points)

1   My mother is o u t g o i n g . She's not s ___ .

2   My older sister is h _ _ _ _ _ _ _ _ _ _ _ g.   She's not l_ _ _ _ .

3   My brother is not s_ _ _ _ _ _ s.   He's f_ _ _ _ _ _ .

4   My dog is f_ _ _ _ _ _ _ _ .   He's not q_ _ _ _ .

Your score: _____ / 12

BONUS: Work with a partner. Think of more personality words.

Ensemble *A perfect family*

LINE-UP

1 → **TODAY'S GOAL:** "Shadow" with 3 people

Shadow = Listen and repeat.

(1st person for 90 seconds, 2nd for 75 seconds, 3rd for 60 seconds)

How do you spell that?

?

A Perfect Family

2 **Language Models** ⊙ CD-1 **track 59** Listen and complete.

A perfect *f* _ _ _ _ _ ? *L* _ _ me see.

A perfect mother is *b* _ _, powerful and *f* _ _ _ _ _.

A perfect father is *t* _ _ _, a non-smoker and *l* _ _ _ _ _ sports.

My perfect sister is ... um well ... _ _ sister! I don't *n* _ _ _ a sister.

My perfect brother is very *p* _ _ _ _ _ _ _.

This is _ _ perfect family. *H* _ _ about *y* _ _?

3 **Think Time**

What is a "perfect family"? Plan your talk. Make notes.

1 _____

2 _____

3 _____

4 _____

IDEAS TO HELP YOU

- healthy
- strong
- pretty / not so pretty
- a good cook
- older / younger
- funny or interesting
- friendly
- a working mother

4 **Action** Stand up. Make 2 lines.

Face your partner. Talk about a perfect family. "Shadow" your partner.

Remember *TODAY'S GOAL!*
Your teacher will check the time.

Change partners like this:

... all musicians!

All musicians? SHADOW SHADOW SHADOW SHADOW

5

How did I do?

	90	75	60
I did very well.	☐	☐	☐
I did well.	☐	☐	☐
I did OK.	☐	☐	☐
I had trouble.	☐	☐	☐
I had BIG trouble!	☐	☐	☐

Now fill in the progress chart on page 121.

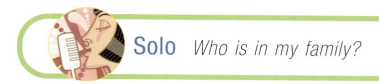
1 Read about these families. Fill in the blanks. There are two extra words.

| grandmother | ~~three~~ | works | big | go | years | play | brothers | lives |

This is Todd and his family from Australia.

There are __three__ people in my family. There is my grandmother, my mother and me. My mum _____ in an office in the city. My _____ works, too. She teaches aerobics!

This is Maria and her family from Mexico.

My family is _____. I have three sisters and two _____. My oldest sister, Linda, is 28. She works. She makes software. My brothers, David and Luis, _____ to elementary school. My two sisters, Celia and Alicia, are 6 and 2. They're lucky. They just eat, sleep, and _____ all day.

2 CD-1 **tracks 60-61** Now listen. Check your answers.

3 **My writing:** Who is in **your** family? What do they do? Think about your family. Write about it.

 If you need help with any new English words, just ask!

On Your Own

- Extra Listening, page 124. Self-Study CD, tracks 30-32.
- Conversation. Listen and repeat. Self-Study CD, track 33.
- Solo. Listen and read. Self-Study CD, track 34.
- Language Check, Solo, Extra Practice www.efcafe.com.

unit 6 I love shoes!

 Preview

1 CD-1 **track 62** Listen. Point to the pictures.

clothes and accessories

t-shirt

shirt

sweater

sweatshirt

jacket

dress

skirt

jeans

shorts

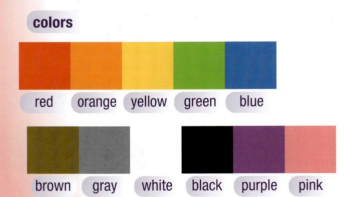
shoes

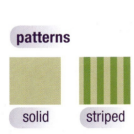
belt

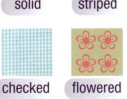
bag

materials

denim

wool

leather

polyester

cotton

colors

red orange yellow green blue

brown gray white black purple pink

patterns

solid striped

checked flowered

2 Listen again. Say the words.

3 Practice with a partner.

Do you have a leather jacket? —⌐• Yeah, it's really cool.
                              ⌊• No, but I want one.

1 CD-1 **tracks 63-68** Look at the pictures. Listen. Which clothing are they talking about? Number the pictures 1-6. There is one extra.

2 Listen again. What do they say about the clothing? Check (✓) two words for each.

1	2	3	4	5	6
✔ sports	☐ long	☐ hot	☐ black	☐ wool	☐ plain
☐ blue	☐ flowered	☐ blue	☐ expensive	☐ cotton	☐ cheap
☐ cool	☐ checked	☐ cotton	☐ cheap	☐ bright	☐ comfortable
☐ cloth	☐ pretty	☐ white	☐ designer brand	☐ cool	☐ designer

About You CD-1 **track 69** Listen and answer.

1. _____

2. _____

3. _____

Compare answers with a partner.

Conversation *It's on sale.*

1 CD-1 **track 70** Listen. Two friends are shopping in a department store.

I like this.

You have ten shirts like that.

sweaters **sweater**
t-shirts **t-shirt**

Aw. But I like this kind of shirt.

Um, how much is it?

It's on sale.

How much?

cheap

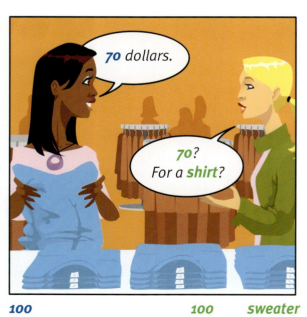

70 dollars.

70? For a shirt?

100 **100** **sweater**
125 **125** **t-shirt**

2 Practice with a partner. Use the **blue** and **green** words.

3 Make your own conversation. Use your ideas.

Pronunciation   ⊙ CD-1 **track 71**   Listen. Repeat silently. Then repeat out loud.

Do you have any **jack**ets?	We have a **lot**. What **kind** would you **like**?
A **leath**er one.	**Here** you are.
How **much** is it?	**Fif**ty dollars.
OK. I'll **take** it.	
I'm looking for some **jeans**.	What **kind**?
Some **Le**vi's®.	**Sor**ry, we're all **out**.

Did you say 15 or 50?

---

1   **Think Time**   You work in a clothing store. You have these clothes. You have one type of each. Check (✓) the one you have.
How much do they cost? Write a price for each. Use your country's money.

jackets
☐ denim
☐ leather
price:

t-shirts
☐ cotton
☐ polyester
price:

sweatshirts
☐ red
☐ blue
price:

skirts
☐ striped
☐ checked
price:

dresses
☐ flowered
☐ solid
price:

shorts
☐ white
☐ orange
price:

sweaters
☐ cotton
☐ wool
price:

shoes
☐ sports
☐ leather
price:

belts
☐ black
☐ brown
price:

bags
☐ large
☐ small
price:

---

2   **B** is a shopper. You are a store clerk. Ask: *May I help you?* Do you have the things **B** wants? Circle the things you sell.

3   Now change. You are the shopper. **B** is the clerk. Try to buy all the things you did NOT check (✓). What do you buy? Write the clothes and the prices.

Clothes	Price

☽ Challenge!
Close your books. With **B**, how many kinds of clothes can you remember?
There are some leather jackets, and...

57

Duet B *May I help you?*

Pronunciation ⊙ CD-1 **track 71** Listen. Repeat silently. Then repeat out loud.

Do you have any **jack**ets?	We have a **lot**. What **kind** would you **like**?
A **leath**er one.	**Here** you are.
How **much** is it?	**Fif**ty dollars.
OK. I'll **take** it.	
I'm looking for some **jeans**.	What **kind**?
Some Le**vi's**®.	**Sor**ry, we're all **out**.

Did you say 15 or 50?

1 **Think Time** You work in a clothing store. You have these clothes. You have one type of each. Check (✓) the one you have.
How much do they cost? Write a price for each. Use your country's money.

jackets
☐ denim
☐ leather
price:

t-shirts
☐ cotton
☐ polyester
price:

sweatshirts
☐ red
☐ blue
price:

skirts
☐ striped
☐ checked
price:

dresses
☐ flowered
☐ solid
price:

shorts
☐ white
☐ orange
price:

sweaters
☐ cotton
☐ wool
price:

shoes
☐ sports
☐ leather
price:

belts
☐ black
☐ brown
price:

bags
☐ large
☐ small
price:

2 Now you are the shopper. **A** is the store clerk. Try to buy all the things you did NOT check (✓). What do you buy? Write the clothes and the prices.

Clothes	Price

3 Now change. **A** is a shopper. You are a clerk. Ask: *May I help you?* Do you have the things **A** wants? Circle the things you sell.

🔄 **Challenge!**
Close your books. With **A**, how many kinds of clothes can you remember?
There are some leather jackets, and...

1 **Grammar Target:** "Some" and "any" with plural nouns

QUESTIONS: use *any*	ANSWERS: Positive	Negative
*Do you have **any** sweatshirts?*	*Yes, we have **some**.*	*No, we don't have **any**.*
STATEMENTS: use **some**	ANSWERS: Positive	Negative
*I am looking for **some** t-shirts.*	*We have **some**.*	*Sorry, we don't have **any**.*

2 **Grammar Check:** *Asking for help at a clothing store*
Circle the correct word. (8 points)

1 A: Do you have (**any** / **a**) black leather jackets?

B: Yes, we have (**it** / **some**) over here. What's your size?

2 A: I'm looking for (**some** / **any**) blue jeans.

B: We have (**any** / **some**) over there.

3 A: Do you have (**any** / **the**) striped shirts?

B: Yes, we do. There are (**any** / **some**) right here.
What color would you like?

4 A: I'm looking for (**any** / **some**) blue cotton shorts.
Do you have (**any** / **this**)?

B: Blue cotton shorts? No, we don't have (**any** / **some**).

3 **Vocabulary Check:** *Clothes*
Write the clothing name. There are two extra words. (4 points)

sweater shoes bags shorts jeans belt skirts

1 These are made of denim and you wear them on your legs: *jeans*

2 You wear this around the top of your pants: _____

3 You wear these on your feet: _____

4 In the summer, you work out in these: _____

5 Women wear these: _____

Your score: _____ / 12

BONUS: Work with a partner. What is your partner wearing? Do you know all the words in English?

Ensemble *I don't like these clothes.*

MIXER

1 → **TODAY'S GOAL:** Have conversations with 4 or more people

2 **Language Models** ◎ CD-1 **track 72** Listen and complete.

W h __ __   c l o t h __ __ don't ___ like?

I don't like ⌐s h___ skirts.

And I don't like polyester clothes. They're too h__ __.

How a___ ___ you?

What c o___ clothes don't you like?

I don't like p___. It's t__ cute.

How about b___ s' clothes?

How about __ __ clothes?

Excuse me?

3 **Think Time** What clothes don't your classmates like? Plan your questions.

1 _____

2 _____

3 _____

4 _____

IDEAS TO HELP YOU

- designer clothes
- used clothing
- my mother's clothes
- too expensive
- too common
- not comfortable
- uncool
- baggy

4 **Action** Stand up. Interview someone.
Check a box. ☑
Move. Interview someone else.

Remember **TODAY'S GOAL!**

- [ ] 1st person
- [ ] 2nd person
- [ ] 3rd person
- [ ] 4th person

Even more people? ☐ ☐ ☐

5 **How did I do?**

- [ ] I did very well.
- [ ] I did well.
- [ ] I did OK.
- [ ] I had trouble.
- [ ] I had BIG trouble!

Now fill in the progress chart on page 121.

1 Read about Man-yi and Sam. Fill in the blanks. There are two extra words.

~~shopping~~   sweater   two   shirt   shops   fun   five   real

This is Man-yi from China.

I like ___shopping___ on the internet. Internet auction sites are fun. This is a Louis Vuitton wallet. This wallet is only _____ dollars. Is it _____ ?

This is Sam from Taiwan.

I like shopping in Hong Kong. There are great _____. It's _____. This is a really cool _____. The price is great too. Who needs the internet?

2 ◎ CD-1 **tracks 73-74** Now listen. Check your answers.

3 ***My writing:*** Where do **you** shop? Who with? What do you buy? Think about your ideas. Write about them.

 Now you can go shopping in English!

On Your Own

- Extra Listening, page 124. Self-Study CD, tracks 35-40.
- Conversation. Listen and repeat. Self-Study CD, track 41.
- Solo. Listen and read. Self-Study CD, track 42.
- Language Check, Solo, Extra Practice www.efcafe.com.

1 Work with a partner.
Choose a word. Think of a sentence with that word. Say the sentence.
Don't say the word. Say BLANK.
Partner, guess the word. Count your partner's guesses.

Check (✔) your partner's guesses.

Our teacher is BLANK.

Serious? Smart?

ruler (page 30)

friendly (46)

younger (46)

camera (30)

listen (14)

finish (38)

midnight (38)

phone number (25)

noon (38)

on-line (39)

sweatshirt (54)

read (17)

drawer (33)

jeans (54)

serious (46)

older (46)

hometown (25)

work out (38)

go (19)

outgoing (46)

sweater (54)

surf (14)

notebook (30)

smart (46)

underline (22)

start (38)

play (19)

first name (27)

last name (27)

cross out (22)

denim (54)

lamp (30)

wallet (30)

leather (54)

You will review *English Firsthand Access*, Units 1–6 and Unit Zero.

Unit Zero

Work with **B**. Do you remember these sentences?

What   *does*   *(that)*   *mean*?
H___ ___ ____ *s* ____?
W___ (____) ___ *E*____?
P_____?
E____ ___?
I'__ _____?

Unit 1: How are you?

Ask **B**. Write **B**'s answers.

What do you like to do in your free time? _____
Where are you from? _____
Do you like music? What kind? _____
Who is your favorite actor? _____
What is your favorite food? _____

Answer **B**'s questions.

Unit 2: Write your name.

Say these instructions. **B** will do them.

Write your last name.
Spell your hometown. I'll write: _____
Circle the number "2."
Draw a car.
Say these letters quickly: L T R D W
Say the months (January to December) quickly.

Follow **B**'s instructions.

Unit 3: What's in your room?

Does **B** have these things? How many? Where? Ask **B**.

_____ a laptop   _____ a lamp
_____ a red shirt   _____ a brother
_____ a blue notebook

Unit 4: When do you get up?

Ask what time **B** does these things. Say what time you do. Who does them earlier? Circle "me" or **B**.

Gets up.	me	B
Eats breakfast.	me	B
Goes home.	me	B
Takes a bath or shower.	me	B

Unit 5: Is your sister shy?

1 Tell **B** about your family. Say 3-5 things about each person.
2 Listen to **B.** Try to remember.
3 What does **B** remember about your family?
4 What do you remember about **B**'s family? Say everything you remember.

Unit 6: I love shoes!

What are your favorite clothes? Tell **B**. Listen to **B**. Ask many questions.

CONGRATULATIONS!

You are really using English, firsthand.

You have ACCESS!

You will review *English Firsthand Access*, Units 1–6 and Unit Zero.

Unit Zero

Work with **A**. Do you remember these sentences?

<u>What</u> <u>does</u> <u>(that)</u> <u>mean</u> ?
<u>H</u>___ ___ ____ <u>s</u>____ ____?
<u>W</u>____ (____) ___ <u>E</u>_____?
<u>P</u>____?
<u>E</u>___ ___?
<u>I'</u>_ _____?

Unit 1: How are you?

Ask **A**. Write **A**'s answers.
 Where are you from? _____
 What do you like to do in your free time? _____
 Who is your favorite actor? _____
 Who is your favorite singer? _____
 Do you like sports? Which ones? _____
Answer **A**'s questions.

Unit 2: Write your name.

Follow **A**'s instructions.
Say these instructions. **A** will do them.
 Write your first name.
 Spell your last name. I'll write: _____
 Cross out the number "2."
 Draw a tree.
 Say these letters quickly: B F H V P
 Say the days (Sunday to Saturday) quickly.

Unit 3: What's in your room?

Does **A** have these things? How many? Where? Ask **A**.

_____ a computer   _____ a red pen
_____ a dictionary   _____ a sister
_____ an orange shirt

Unit 4: When do you get up?

Ask what time **A** does these things. Say what time you do. Who does them earlier? Circle "me" or **A**.

Goes to school / work.	me	A
Eats dinner.	me	A
Turns off the TV / stereo, etc.	me	A
Goes to bed.	me	A

Unit 5: Is your sister shy?

1 Listen to **A**. Try to remember.
2 Tell **A** about your family. Say 3-5 things about each person.
3 What do you remember about **A**'s family? Say everything you remember.
4 What does **A** remember about your family?

Unit 6: I love shoes!

A will talk about clothes. Listen. Ask many questions.
What are your favorite clothes? Tell **A**.

CONGRATULATIONS!

You are really using English, firsthand.

You have ACCESS!

Let's Talk: *A conversation game*

This is a speaking game. Work in groups of 3 or 4.

1 (**Think Time**) Look at the questions. Which are interesting? Decide on 5 (or more) to answer. Circle them. What will you say? Think about your answers.

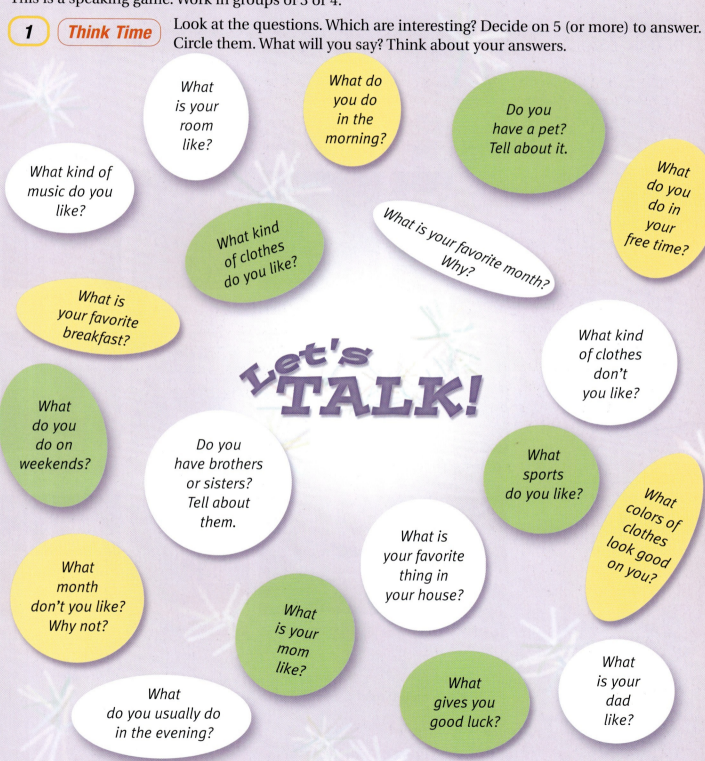

What is your room like?

What do you do in the morning?

Do you have a pet? Tell about it.

What kind of music do you like?

What do you do in your free time?

What kind of clothes do you like?

What is your favorite month? Why?

What is your favorite breakfast?

What kind of clothes don't you like?

Let's TALK!

What do you do on weekends?

Do you have brothers or sisters? Tell about them.

What sports do you like?

What colors of clothes look good on you?

What month don't you like? Why not?

What is your favorite thing in your house?

What is your mom like?

What do you usually do in the evening?

What gives you good luck?

What is your dad like?

2 Play the game. Put a space marker on a question. Answer it. Give long answers. Partners, ask questions. Take turns. Enjoy your conversation.

unit 7   I love weekends!

 Preview

1   CD-2 **track 1**   Listen. Point to the pictures.

listen to music

go to karaoke

go out for dinner

go to concerts

go to the movies

go shopping

do homework

watch DVDs

talk on your cell phone

surf the internet

practice English

hang out with your friends

2   Listen again. Say the phrases.

3   Practice with a partner.

Do you ... ? — *Yes, I do. / Yes, always. / Yes, sometimes.*
              — *No, I don't. / No, never.*

Listening *How often?*

1 ⊚ CD-2 **tracks 2-4**   Listen. Order the activities. Write 1, 2, 3 for each person.

1 Kate
- ☐ sing in the band
- ☐ give concerts
- ☐ 1 have band practice

2 Koji
- ☐ go to the movies
- ☐ hang out with friends
- ☐ go to karaoke

3 Manee
- ☐ sleep late
- ☐ study
- ☐ go shopping

2   Listen to the conversations. Write always, usually, often, sometimes, hardly ever, or never.

Always	Usually	Often	Sometimes	Hardly ever	Never

This is Kate.

- *often* — have band practice
- — give concerts
- — sing in the band

This is Koji.

- — hang out with friends
- — go to movies
- — go to karaoke

This is Manee.

- — sleep late on Saturday morning
- — go shopping on Sunday afternoon
- — study on Sunday evening.

About You   ⊚ CD-2 **track 5**   Listen and answer.

1. _____

2. _____

3. _____

Compare answers with a partner.

Conversation *Every weekend!*

1 CD-2 **track 6** Listen. Two people are on their first date.

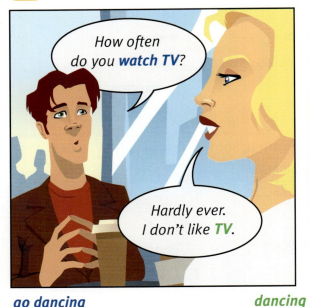

> How often do you **watch TV**?
>
> Hardly ever. I don't like **TV**.

go dancing
go to karaoke   *dancing*
                                     karaoke

> How often do you **go to the movies**?
>
> Every **weekend**. I love **movies**!

listen to music   *day*   *music*
play sports   *week*   *sports*

> What kind of **movies** do you like?
>
> I usually **watch comedies**.

music   *listen to rock*
sports   *play tennis*

> **Comedies**! Me, too!
>
> *Cool*.

Rock   *Great*
Tennis   *Ah! Good!*

2 Practice with a partner. Use the **blue** and *green* words.

3 Make your own conversation. Use your ideas.

Pronunciation   CD-2 **track 7** Listen. Repeat silently. Then repeat out loud.

How **of**ten do you	go **shop**ping	on **week**ends?		I	**of**ten	do.
	practice **Eng**lish	on **week**days?			**some**times	
	go to the **mo**vies	on **Sat**urdays?			**ne**ver	

1 (**Think Time**) Answer the questions about yourself. Mark your answers.

	Your answers				B's answers			
How often do you ...	Always / Almost always	Often	Sometimes	Never / Hardly ever	Always / Almost always	Often	Sometimes	Never / Hardly ever
1 ... go out to dinner on weekends?								
2 ... buy new clothes at department stores?								
3 ... listen to music in the evening?								
4 ... practice English at lunch time?								
5 ... hang out with your friends after school?								
6 ... go to the movies on weekends?								
7 ... do your homework before class?								
8 ... surf the internet at night?								
9 ... go to concerts on Saturday night?								

Pardon?

2 Ask **B** the questions.
Mark **B**'s answers.
Then say your answers.

How often do you listen to music? *Always!*

Challenge!
Make your own questions for **B**.

Duet B *I often do.*

Pronunciation   CD-2 **track 7** Listen. Repeat silently. Then repeat out loud.

How **of**ten do you	go **shop**ping	on **week**ends?	I	**of**ten	do.
	practice **Eng**lish	on **week**days?		**some**times	
	go to the **mo**vies	on **Sa**turdays?		**nev**er	

1 **Think Time** Answer the questions about yourself. Mark your answers.

How often do you ...	Your answers				A's answers			
	Always / Almost always	Often	Sometimes	Never / Hardly ever	Always / Almost always	Often	Sometimes	Never / Hardly ever
1 ... cook dinner in the evening?								
2 ... go shopping on Sundays?								
3 ... use your cell phone in class?								
4 ... practice English at lunch time?								
5 ... play sports on school vacations?								
6 ... watch DVDs at night?								
7 ... speak English in this class?								
8 ... go dancing on Friday night?								
9 ... watch TV at night?								

Pardon?

2 Answer **A**'s questions. Then ask **A** the questions. Mark **A**'s answers.

How often do you listen to music?

Hardly ever!

Challenge!
Make your own questions for **A**.

Language Check

1 Grammar Target: Frequency adverbs

frequency adverb	+	verb	
She	always	sleeps	late on Saturday.
They	often	go	shopping after school.

	verb BE	+	frequency adverb	
He	is		always	tired.
They	are		never	late.

Look at the order of the words:
frequency adverb **before** the verb,
but frequency adverb **after** "is" / "are" / "am"

2 Grammar Check: Habits and routines Put the words in the correct order. (5 points)

1 cleans never his room Jin on weekends
  Jin _never_ _cleans_ _his_ _room_ _on_ _weekends_ .

2 Saturdays on Kate dancing goes sometimes
  _____ _sometimes_ _____ _____ _____ _____ .

3 after are hungry they school usually
  _____ _____ _usually_ _____ _____ _____ .

4 Mari late is for class ever hardly
  _____ ____ _hardly_ _ever_ _____ _____ _____ .

5 always in class I am sleepy
  ___ ____ _always_ _____ _____ _____ .

6 cooks on usually Sunday she night dinner
  _____ _usually_ _____ _____ _____ _____ _____ .

3 Vocabulary Check: Weekend activities Write *go*, *go to*, or *play*. (7 points)

A Do you want to _go to_ the movies on Friday night?
B Sorry, I always _____ video games with my friends on Fridays.

A OK. How about Saturday? Do you want to _____ karaoke?
B I can't. I always _____ out to dinner with my roommates on Saturdays.

A Well, do you want to _____ shopping on Sunday afternoon?
B I'm sorry. I _____ soccer every Sunday at 2:00.

A What about Sunday night? Do you want to _____ dancing?
B Sunday night? I usually _____ cards with my family.

A You're really busy!
B Sorry.

Your score: _____ / 12

BONUS: Work with a partner. Think of 2 more phrases with *go*, *go to*, and *play*.

Ensemble *My weekend? Let me see...*

MIXER

1 → **TODAY'S GOAL: Chat with 4 or more people**

2 **Language Models** ◎ CD-2 **track 8** Listen and complete.

Excuse _m e_ , what do you do on _w_ _ _ _ _ _ _ _?

Let _ _ see. I _ _ _ out.

_W h_ _ _ _ do you _ _?

_ _ _ _ town.

_W h_ _ with?

My _f_ _ _ _ _ _ _ .

Anything else?

I sometimes _w_ _ _ _ _ _ _m_ _ _ _ _. How about you?

I'm sorry?

3 **Think Time** What do your classmates do on the weekend? Plan your questions.

1 _____

2 _____

3 _____

4 _____

IDEAS TO HELP YOU

• **relax at home**
• **meet friends**
• **study English**
• **clean my room**
• **work / sleep!**
• **in the city**
• **at my friend's house**
• **my family**

4 **Action** Stand up. Chat to someone.
Check a box. ☑
Move. Chat to someone else.

Remember **TODAY'S GOAL!**

☐ 1st person

☐ 2nd person

☐ 3rd person

☐ 4th person

Even more people? ☐ ☐ ☐

5

How did I do?

☐ I did very well.
☐ I did well.
☐ I did OK.
☐ I had trouble.
☐ I had BIG trouble!

Now fill in the progress chart on page 121.

Solo *What do you do on weekends?*

1 Read about these students. Fill in the spaces. There are two extra words.

surfer	museums	~~shopping~~	waves	wear
clothes	park	college	paintings	get up

This is Yukari, Eri, and Sayaka.
Tokyo, Japan

We almost always go
shopping in Tokyo
on weekends. We love
_____!
Sometimes we _____
crazy clothes.

This is Suzanne.
Perth, Australia

I'm a _____. On the weekends, I
often wake up at 5 am. The _____
are great early in the morning. Surf's up!

This is Keeyong.
Seoul, Korea

I never _____ before noon on
weekends. I usually go out to art galleries or
_____ in the afternoon. Sometimes
I work on my own _____.

2 ⊚ CD-2 **tracks 9-11** Now listen. Check your answers.

3 **My writing:** Now write about **your** weekend.
Use these words:

on weekends   always   usually   sometimes

  Have a good weekend — in English!

On Your Own

- Extra Listening, page 125. Self-Study CD, tracks 43-45.
- Conversation. Listen and repeat. Self-Study CD, track 46.
- Solo. Listen and read. Self-Study CD, track 47
- Language Check, Solo, Extra Practice www.efcafe.com.

Preview

1   CD-2 **track 12**   Listen. Point to the pictures.

fruit
- bananas
- mangoes
- strawberries

vegetables
- corn
- beans
- mushrooms
- peppers
- onions
- tomatoes

lunch
- pizza
- sandwiches
- bread
- rice
- salad
- eggs

dinner
- beef
- fish
- sausage
- chicken

barbecue
- mustard
- salsa
- barbecue sauce
- hot dog buns
- ice cream
- potato chips

2   Listen again. Say the words.

3   Practice with a partner.

1 CD-2 **tracks 13-18**   People are shopping for food. Listen. What foods are they talking about? Number the pictures 1-6. There are three extra pictures.

chicken   salsa   tomatoes

bread   eggs   coffee

sausages   bananas   soda

2 Listen again. How much do they buy? Write the number.

1 [1] loaf (loaves)   4 [   ] carton(s)

2 [   ]   5 [   ] bottle(s)

3 [   ] grams   6 [   ]

About You   CD-2 **track 19**   Listen and answer.

1. _____

2. _____

3. _____

Compare answers with a partner.

Conversation *What do we need for the party?*

1 CD-2 **track 20** Listen. Roommates are in a supermarket.

ice cream **coke**

A lot.
A little.

cups
napkins

Oops!

2 Practice with a partner. Use the **blue** and *green* words.

3 Make your own conversation. Use your ideas.

Duet A *Planning a barbecue*

Pronunciation   CD-2 **track 21** Listen. Repeat silently. Then repeat out loud.

Do **you** have any	**on**ions?	I have some. **Here** you are.
	mangoes?	I have **ten**.
	chicken?	About **3**oo **grams**.
	po**ta**to chips?	**Sor**ry, I **don't**.

Pardon?

1 (**Think Time**) Cut (✂) or tear all the cards on page 119 from one book.
Look at the pictures. How do you say the food in English?

2 Put all the cards face-down on the table.

3 **A** chooses a blue card. Ask the question.
B chooses a pink card.
If the food is the same, **B** says how many:
"Yes. I have 10."
A gets both cards.

If the food is different, say, *"No, I don't
have any."* Put both cards back.
Take turns.

Do you have
any tomatoes?

↻ Challenge!

What else do you need for a party? Make a list.
What do you already have?
How many other foods can you name in English?

Duet B *Planning a barbecue*

Pronunciation CD-2 **track 21** Listen. Repeat silently. Then repeat out loud.

Do **you** have any	**on**ions?	*I have some.* **Here** *you are.*
	mangoes?	*I have* **ten.**
	chicken?	*About* **3**00 **grams.**
	po**ta**to chips?	**Sorry, I don't.**

Pardon?

1 (**Think Time**) Cut (✂) or tear all the cards on page 119 from one book.
Look at the pictures. How do you say the food in English?

2 Put all the cards face-down on the table.

3 **A** chooses a blue card. **A** asks the question.
B chooses a pink card.
If the food is the same, **B** says how many:
"Yes. I have 10."
A gets both cards.

If the food is different, say, *"No, I don't have any."* Put both cards back.
Take turns.

Do you have any tomatoes?

↻ Challenge!

What else do you need for a party? Make a list.
What do you already have?
How many other foods can you name in English?

Language Check

1 **Grammar Target:** *Count and non-count nouns many, much, a little, a few*

QUESTIONS: *count nouns*	ANSWERS: *count nouns*
How many **tomatoes** *do we have?*	*We have* **a few**.
bananas *do we have?*	**some** / **a lot**.
QUESTIONS: **non-count nouns**	ANSWERS: **non-count nouns**
How much **milk** *do we have?*	*We have* **a little**.
mustard *do we have?*	**some** / **a lot**.

Count nouns = things you can **count** (apples, peppers, mushrooms)

Non-count nouns = things you **can't count** (water, rice, barbecue sauce)

2 **Grammar Check:** *Going shopping*   Write *many*, *much*, *a few* or *a little*. (7 points)

1 A: I'm going shopping. What do we need?

 B: Let's see. How __many__ onions do we have?

2 A: We only have _____. I'll get some more.

 B: How _____ coffee do we have?

3 A: There is _____. Do you want some more?

 B: Yes. How _____ rice is there?

4 A: We have _____. I'll get another bag.

 B: Oh. How about bananas? How _____ do we have?

5 A: We have _____. Let's get another bunch.
   I eat them every day.

 B: You're so healthy!

3 **Vocabulary Check:** *Food*
One word does not fit. Circle the word. (5 points)

1 mangoes bananas (spicy) apples

2 corn mushrooms onions breakfast

3 soda chicken coffee tea

4 bread plates cups napkins

5 chicken ice cream sausage fish

6 breakfast lunch dinner salad

Your score: _____ / 12

BONUS: What food does your partner have at home right now?
Ask: *"Do you have any..."* *"How many / much... do you have?"*

Ensemble *My favorite meal*

GROUP TALK

1 → **TODAY'S GOAL:** Ask 3 questions to ALL your group.

2 **Language Models** CD-2 **track 22** Listen and complete.

What's your favorite *m* _ _ _?

I love *b* _ _ _ _ _ _ _ _ _ .

What do you eat for breakfast?

E _ _ _ and spicy sausages.

I eat them with *s* _ _ _ _ _.

What's that?

It's made from *t* _ _ _ _ _ _ _ _ and onions.

3 **Think Time** Plan your questions. Make notes.

1 _____

2 _____

3 _____

IDEAS TO HELP YOU

- lunch
- dinner
- snacks
- dessert
- sweet

4 **Action** Make a group of 3-4.
Ask your questions.
Listen to the answers. React to the answers.

Remember **TODAY'S GOAL!**

5 How did I do?
- ☐ I did very well.
- ☐ I did well.
- ☐ I did OK.
- ☐ I had trouble.
- ☐ I had BIG trouble!

Now fill in the progress chart on page 121.

Solo *Can you eat 67 hamburgers?*

1 Read about Takeru and Brian. Fill in the blanks. There are two extra words.

fries	eats	don't	eater
hamburgers	healthy	~~weighs~~	good

This is Takeru Kobayashi from Japan.

He *weighs* 59 kilos and is 170 cm tall. He can eat 67 _____ in 20 minutes. He can also eat 49 hot dogs in 12 minutes. It's amazing. Takeru is the world's greatest _____ .

This is Brian from the U.S.

I like fast food. I love _____ . But fast food is not _____ so I only eat it at lunchtime. My lunch is two or three hamburgers, large fries and a Coke®, then an apple pie to finish. I _____ eat so much at lunchtime.

2 ⊙ CD-2 **tracks 23-24** Now listen. Check your answers.

3 **My writing:** Do **you** eat fast food?
What do you eat for lunch?
Think about it. Write about it.

Think of English words for food the next time you're shopping!

On Your Own

- Extra Listening, page 125. Self-Study CD, tracks 48-53.
- Conversation. Listen and repeat. Self-Study CD, track 54.
- Solo. Listen and read. Self-Study CD, track 55.
- Language Check, Solo, Extra Practice www.efcafe.com.

unit 9 What are they doing?

1 CD-2 **track 25** Listen. Point to the pictures.

running

snowboarding

playing basketball

jumping

swimming

talking on the phone

bowling

practicing judo

lifting weights

playing soccer

playing tennis

boxing

watching

2 Listen again. Say the words and phrases.

3 Work in groups of 3. Then 2 people close your books.
One person gives a hint. Partners, guess.
5 people.   *Playing basketball.*

1 ⊚ CD-2 **tracks 26-33**   Listen. What are they doing? Number the pictures 1-8. There is one extra.

○

○

○

○

○

①

○

○

○

2   Who is doing the action? Check (✓) the person.

1	☐ sister	✓ grandmother		5	☐ brother	☐ sister
2	☐ brother	☐ father		6	☐ father	☐ grandfather
3	☐ mother	☐ sister		7	☐ brother	☐ father
4	☐ friend	☐ teacher		8	☐ sister	☐ mother

About You

⊚ CD-2 **track 34**   Listen and answer.

1. _____

2. _____

3. _____

Compare answers with a partner.

83

Conversation *What's everyone doing?*

1 CD-2 **track 35** Listen. A study-abroad student is calling home.

Hi, Mom.

*Hi! How is **Sydney**?*

Great! But I miss you.

What's everyone doing right now?

**Buenos Aires
Hong Kong** **Cool**

*Well, your father's **playing tennis**.*

**reading the newspaper
watching TV**

*What about **Meg**?*

*She's hanging out with **her** friends.*

Jack **He's** **his**

I really miss Max.

What's he doing?

*Your dog is **sleeping**, of course.*

eating

2 Practice with a partner. Use the **blue** and **green** words.

3 Make your own conversation. Use your ideas.

Pronunciation ⊚ CD-2 **track 36** Listen. Repeat silently. Then repeat out loud.

Is	he	**watch**ing a **mov**ie?	That's **right**.
	she	**prac**ticing ka**ra**te?	Not e**xact**ly.
Are	they	**figh**ting?	**No**, they're **do**ing something **else**.
			Good **guess**!

How do you say _____ in English?

1 (**Think Time**) Look at the green pictures. What do you think the people are doing?

1 He is _____

2 She's playing tennis.
B's guesses: ☐1 ☐2 ☐3

3 They're _____

4 She's using a computer.
B's guesses: ☐1 ☐2 ☐3

5 He's _____

6 They're practicing judo.
B's guesses: ☐1 ☐2 ☐3

7 He's _____

8 They're _____

9 She's bowling.
B's guesses: ☐1 ☐2 ☐3

10 She's jumping rope.
B's guesses: ☐1 ☐2 ☐3

11 He's _____

12 She's playing soccer.
B's guesses: ☐1 ☐2 ☐3

13 He's _____

14 She's skydiving.
B's guesses: ☐1 ☐2 ☐3

15 Your idea:_____
(draw or act out)

2 What are the people in green doing? Guess.
Answer **B**'s questions. **B** cannot see the gray information.

↺ **Challenge!**
Close your book. There were 15 ideas.
How many can you remember?

Duet B *What are they doing?*

Pronunciation   CD-2 **track 36**   Listen. Repeat silently. Then repeat out loud.

Is	he	*watch*ing a *mov*ie?	That's **right**.
	she	*prac*ticing ka*ra*te?	Not ex**act**ly.
Are	they	*fight*ing?	**No**, they're **do**ing something **else**.
			Good **guess**!

How do you say _____ in English?

1   **Think Time**   Look at the blue pictures. What do you think the people are doing?

1 He is throwing a ball.
A's guesses: ☐1 ☐2 ☐3

2 She is _____

3 They're dancing.
A's guesses: ☐1 ☐2 ☐3

4 She's _____

5 He's watching TV.
A's guesses: ☐1 ☐2 ☐3

6 They're _____

7 He's talking on a phone.
A's guesses: ☐1 ☐2 ☐3

8 They're singing.
A's guesses: ☐1 ☐2 ☐3

9 She's _____

10 She's _____

11 He's eating.
A's guesses: ☐1 ☐2 ☐3

12 She's _____

13 He's lifting weights.
A's guesses: ☐1 ☐2 ☐3

14 She's _____

15 Your idea: _____
(draw or act out)

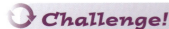

2   What are the people in blue doing? Guess.
Answer **A**'s questions. **A** cannot see the gray information.

Challenge!
Close your book. There were 15 ideas.
How many can you remember?

 Language Check

1   **Grammar Target:** *Present continuous – actions happening now*

BE	+	subject	+	verb + ing	…?	Answers
Is		he		*playing*	soccer?	Yes, he is.
Are		you		*watching*	TV?	No, I'm not. It's a DVD.

question word	+	BE	+	subject	+	verb + ing	…?	Answers
What		**are**		they		*doing?*		They're hanging out.
		is		she		*watching?*		She's watching a movie.
		are		you		*eating?*		I'm eating an apple.

Remember:
is, are + … ing

2   **Grammar Check:** *Actions happening now*   Find the mistakes. Make corrections. (6 points)

1   What he is doing?   *What is he doing?* _____ .

2   She is play tennis. _____ .

3   Is they watching TV? _____ .

4   They practicing English. _____ .

5   I talking on the phone. _____ .

6   What you are making? _____ .

7   They are eat breakfast. _____ .

3   **Vocabulary Check:** *Sports*   Unscramble the letters. (5 points)

1   n b g o i x   *b o x i n g*

2   c r o s e c   _ _ _ _ _ _

3   d j u o   _ _ _ _

4   s n t i n e   _ _ _ _ _ _

5   g i w m n m i s   _ _ _ _ _ _ _ _

6   i n b a g s w n o o r d   _ _ _ _ _ _ _ _ _ _ _

7   w g l o n b i   _ _ _ _ _ _ _

Your score: _____ / 12

BONUS: Work with a partner. How many more sports can you name? Write them down.

GROUP TALK

1 → **TODAY'S GOAL:** Ask 3 questions to ALL your group.

2 **Language Models** ◎ CD-2 track 37 Listen and complete.

Do you like w _ _ _ _ _ _ _ sports on TV?

Is _ _ interesting?

Do you like p _ _ _ _ _ _ sports?

Can you s _ _ _?   Are _ _ _ fast?

Do you like ski_ _ _?   Is _ _ easy?

Are you in good shape?   Is your teacher in good shape?

I don't know, but…umm…maybe…NOT!

3 **Think Time** Plan your questions. Make notes.

1 _____

2 _____

3 _____

IDEAS TO HELP YOU

- **strong / weak**
- **fast / slow**
- **good / not so good**
- **skillful**
- **very skillful**
- **very very skillful!**
- **mother / father, etc.**

4 **Action** Make a group of 3-4.

Ask your questions.
Listen to the answers.
React to the answers: *Great! Why? Why not?*
No way! Really! Really? Are you sure?

Remember **TODAY'S GOAL!**

5

How did I do?

	Speaking	Answering	Reacting
Good.	☐	☐	☐
Not bad.	☐	☐	☐
OK.	☐	☐	☐
Not so good.	☐	☐	☐
I had BIG trouble!	☐	☐	☐

Now fill in the progress chart on page 121.

1 Read about Jodie, Lai-san, and Young Ho. Fill in the spaces. There are two extra words.

red ~~hard~~ sometimes only home away family superstar

This is Jodie from the UK.

I like soccer. I play for Arsenal in England. I play ___hard___. But last week I got a _____ card. Can you believe it?

This is Lai-san from China.

My family is a volleyball _____ . We all like playing volleyball. My father is very tall, but I am _____ 190 cm.

This is Young Ho from Korea.

I like watching baseball. My favorite team is the Lotte Giants. I _____ go to their _____ games in the Sajik Baseball Stadium in Busan.

2 CD-2 **tracks 38-40** Now listen. Check your answers.

3 **My writing:** What sport do **you** play? What sport do you watch? Think about sports. Write about them.

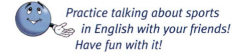

Practice talking about sports in English with your friends! Have fun with it!

On Your Own

- Extra Listening, page 126. Self-Study CD, tracks 56-63.
- Conversation. Listen and repeat. Self-Study CD, track 64.
- Solo. Listen and read. Self-Study CD, track 65.
- Language Check, Solo, Extra Practice www.efcafe.com.

unit 10 My house is not so big.

Preview

1 ⊚ CD-2 **track 41** Listen. Point to the pictures.

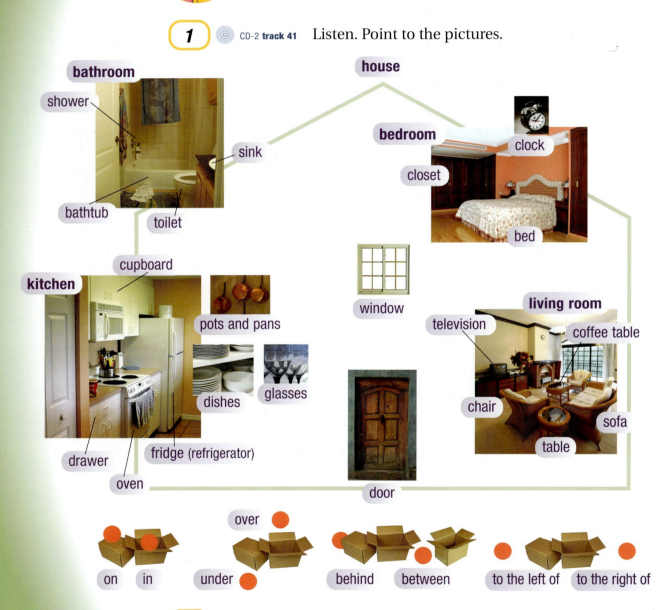

2 Listen again. Say the words.

3 Work in groups of 3. One person says a word. Partners, try to be first to touch it.

1 ○ CD-2 **tracks 42-49** Listen. Put the items in the picture.

2 Listen again. Complete the sentences.

1 The dishes are _over_ the stove _on_ the bottom shelf.

2 The glasses are on the _____ shelf on the _____.

3 The juice is _____ the fridge on the _____ shelf.

4 The forks and spoons are _____ the drawer _____ the sink.

5 The clock is _____ the windows.

6 The bag is _____ the table.

7 Put your glass _____ the sink.

8 The tea is _____ the stove.

About You

○ CD-2 **track 50** Listen and answer.

1. _____

2. _____

3. _____

Compare answers with a partner.

1 CD-2 **track 51** Listen. A friend is moving into a new house.

next to *next to*

in front of
by

in front of
by

2 Practice with a partner. Use the **blue** and **green** words.

3 Make your own conversation. Use your ideas.

Pronunciation   ◎ CD-2 **track 52**   Listen. Repeat silently. Then repeat out loud.

Draw	a **house**	in the **mid**dle.
	a **bird**	on the **car**.
	a small **win**dow	over the **door**.
	two windows	to the **left** of the **door**.
	a **car**	be**tween** the **house** and the **tree**.
There is	a big **hill**	be**hind** the **house**.
There are	**two cats**	**un**der the **tree**.
There is	a **bi**cycle	in **front** of the **house**.

Excuse me?

I don't understand.

1   **Think Time**   Look at the picture. You will tell **B** how to draw it. What will you say?

2   Tell **B** how to draw the picture.

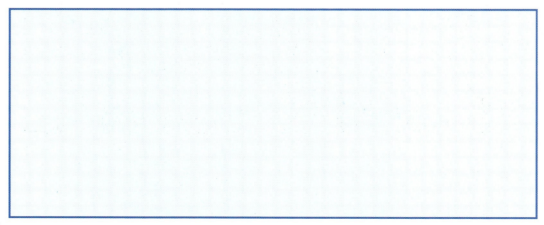

3   Draw **B**'s picture.

Challenge!
Close your book. Draw **B**'s home or room.

Duet B *Can you draw this?*

Pronunciation CD-2 **track 52**   Listen. Repeat silently. Then repeat out loud.

Draw	a **house**	in the **mid**dle.
	a **bird**	on the **car**.
	a small **win**dow	over the **door**.
	two windows	to the **left** of the **door**.
	a **car**	be**tween** the **house** and the **tree**.
There is	a big **hill**	be**hind** the **house**.
There are	**two cats**	**un**der the **tree**.
There is	a **bi**cycle	in **front** of the **house**.

Excuse me?

I don't understand.

1   **Think Time**   Look at the picture. You will tell **A** how to draw it. What will you say?

hill

lake

2   Tell **A** how to draw the picture.

3   Draw **A**'s picture.

◯ Challenge!
Close your book. Draw **A**'s home or room.

1 **Grammar Target:** *Prepositions of location*

The cat and dog	are	*in*	the living room.
The picture	is	*over*	the sofa.
The cat		*under*	
The dog		*on*	
The table		*next to*	
The coffee table		*in front of*	
The window		*behind*	
The plant		*to the right of*	
The lamp		*to the left of*	
The sofa	is	*between*	the table and the plant.

2 **Grammar Check:** *Where is it?* Look at the picture. Finish the sentences. (5 points)

1 The table is ____*in*____ the kitchen.

2 The cat is _____ the table.

3 The pots and pans are _____ the sink.

4 The glasses are _____ the table.

5 The sink is _____ the fridge and the counter.

6 The dog is _____ the fridge.

3 **Vocabulary Check:** *Which room?* Write the words in the boxes. (7 points)

| refrigerator | sofa | coffee table | bathtub |
| toilet | pots and pans | shower | oven |

bathroom	kitchen	living room
toilet		

Your score: _____ / 12

BONUS: Work with a partner. Write 2 more items in each box.

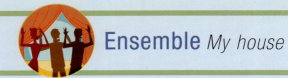

Ensemble *My house*

LINE-UP

1 → **TODAY'S GOAL:** "Shadow" with 3 people
Shadow = Listen and repeat.
(1st person for 120 seconds, 2nd for 90 seconds, 3rd for 75 seconds)

2 **Language Models** ◉ CD-2 **track 53** Listen and complete.

My house is _ _ _ _ _ big.

My room is *c* _ _ _ and a bit *d* _ _ _.

In my house, there is a _ _ _ _ _ _ _ room, *k* _ _ _ _ _ _ _ ,
b _ _ _ room and *3* _ _ _ _ rooms.

I like the bathroom _ _ my house. I love a *h* _ _ _ _ _ _ !

How *a* _ _ _ _ _ you?

3 **Think Time** Plan how to talk about your house. Make notes.

1 _____
2 _____
3 _____
4 _____

IDEAS TO HELP YOU

- **normal size**
- **north / south**
- **east / west**
- **warm / cold**
- **bright / dark**
- **in winter**
- **in summer**
- **colors**
- **messy / neat**

4 **Think Time** Stand up. Make 2 lines.
Face your partner.
Talk about your house.
Shadow your partner.

Remember **TODAY'S GOAL!**
Your teacher will check the time.

Change partners like this:

● ● ● ● ● ●
●→●→●→●→●→●
← ← ← ← ← ←

5

How did I do?

	120	90	75
I did very well.	☐	☐	☐
I did well.	☐	☐	☐
I did OK.	☐	☐	☐
I had trouble.	☐	☐	☐
I had BIG trouble!	☐	☐	☐

Now fill in the progress chart on page 121.

Solo *Is my house old?*

1 Read about the houses in different countries. Fill in the blanks. There are two extra words.

need	Japan	favorite	before
~~England~~	warm	dark	only	living

This is Karen's house.

In ___England___ there are many old houses. But my house is not so old. It was built _____ 100 years ago.

There is a fireplace in my _____ room. So my house is very _____ in winter. I love my house!

This is Ken's apartment.

In _____ most apartments are modern. But mine is old — it was built 30 years ago. I _____ a new apartment.

My apartment is _____ and cold. I want a warm and sunny apartment.

2 CD-2 **tracks 54-55** Now listen. Check your answers.

3 **My writing:** How about houses in **your** country? Think about your ideas. Write about them.

 How many new words can you use?

On Your Own

- Extra Listening, page 127. Self-Study CD, tracks 66-73.
- Conversation. Listen and repeat. Self-Study CD, track 74.
- Solo. Listen and read. Self-Study CD, track 75.
- Language Check, Solo, Extra Practice www.efcafe.com.

unit 11 Where did you go?

1 ◎ CD-2 **track 56** Listen. Point to the pictures.

She spent 2 weeks there.

Last month, Sara took a vacation.   She rode in a plane.   She visited her grandmother and grandfather.

They went to the beach.

It was sunny.

Sara and her grandmother rode a roller coaster.

She played volleyball.   Her grandfather ate a hot dog and watched them.

Sara felt very happy.

They also saw a movie.   Sara bought a t-shirt for her little brother.   She had a good time.

When it was time to go home,

Sara gave her grandmother a big hug.   Sara got a present.   Sara studied on the way home.

2 Listen again. Say the phrases.

3 Practice with a partner. Say a word. Partner, point to the picture. Then close your books. How many can you remember?

1 CD-2 **tracks 57-64** Listen. What did they do? Number the pictures 1-8. There is one extra.

2 Listen again. Listen to their answers. Check (✔) the verbs they say. They may use more than one verb.

1	☐ went	✔ watched	☐ rode		5	☐ went	☐ ate	☐ had
2	☐ spent	☐ felt	☐ went		6	☐ had	☐ watched	☐ went
3	☐ was	☐ had	☐ went		7	☐ studied	☐ was	☐ gave
4	☐ went	☐ was	☐ got		8	☐ rode	☐ felt	☐ saw

About You

CD-2 **track 65** Listen and answer.

1. _____

2. _____

3. _____

Compare answers with a partner.

Conversation *I stayed home.*

1 CD-2 **track 66** Listen. Two friends are talking on Monday morning.

*What did you do **on Friday night**?*

*I **stayed home**.*

last weekend
on Sunday

watched TV
took a walk

Sounds boring.

*Oh, it was **great**.*

fun
not boring

Really?

Yeah.

*I **stayed home** with, uh, a good friend.*

watched TV
took a walk

A friend? Who?

Uh, just a friend.

2 Practice with a partner. Use the **blue** and **green** words.

3 Make your own conversation. Use your ideas.

Pronunciation   ⊚ CD-2 **track 67**   Listen. Repeat silently. Then repeat out loud.

Yesterday,	I went	**shop**ping.
	I **bought**	some **clothes**.
	I spent	**too** much **mon**ey.
Where	did	you **go**?
What	did	you **buy**?

Excuse me?

1   **Think Time**   Look at the verbs. Write the past tense. For more help, see page 98.

watch
watched

work
worked

do
did

visit
_____

study
_____

go
_____

make
_____

see
_____

buy
_____

give
_____

play
_____

be
_____

spend
_____

feel
_____

get
_____

take
_____

eat
_____

have
_____

ride
_____

2   Choose one of the verbs. Say a true past tense sentence. Add two more sentences.

3   Partner, ask questions. Make a check (✓) for each question.
My questions:

Who...?   *What...?*   *When...?*   *Where...?*   *Why...?*
☐☐☐☐☐   ☐☐☐☐☐   ☐☐☐☐☐   ☐☐☐☐☐   ☐☐☐☐☐

How...?   *Did...?*   *Were...?*   *Was...?*
☐☐☐☐☐   ☐☐☐☐☐   ☐☐☐☐☐   ☐☐☐☐☐

↻ **Challenge!**
Choose **B**'s most interesting answer. How many more questions can you ask?

Pronunciation   ◉ CD-2 **track 67**   Listen. Repeat silently. Then repeat out loud.

Yesterday,	*I went*	***shop**ping.*
	*I **bought***	*some **clothes**.*
	I spent	***too** much **mon**ey.*
Where	*did*	*you **go**?*
What	*did*	*you **buy**?*

Excuse me?

1   **Think Time**   Look at the verbs. Write the past tense. For more help, see page 98.

watch
watched

work
worked

do
did

visit
_____

study
_____

go
_____

make
_____

see
_____

buy
_____

give
_____

play
_____

be
_____

spend
_____

feel
_____

get
_____

take
_____

eat
_____

have
_____

ride
_____

2   Choose one of the verbs. Say a true past tense sentence. Add two more sentences.

3   Partner, ask questions. Make a check (✓) for each question.
My questions:

Who...? ☐☐☐☐☐
What...? ☐☐☐☐☐
When...? ☐☐☐☐☐
Where...? ☐☐☐☐☐
Why...? ☐☐☐☐☐

How...? ☐☐☐☐☐
Did...? ☐☐☐☐☐
Were...? ☐☐☐☐☐
Was...? ☐☐☐☐

 **Challenge!**
Choose **A**'s most interesting answer. How many more questions can you ask?

1   Grammar Target: *Past simple tense*

Did + **subject** + *verb*			…?	Answers
Did	you	*take*	a vacation last year?	Yes, I did.
	she			No, she didn't.
question word + *did* + **subject** +			*verb* ?	Answers
Where	*did*	you	*go?*	I went to London.
What	*did*	they	*do?*	They visited their friends.
(Be) + **subject** + …?				Answers
Were	you		in England last year?	Yes, I was.
	they			Yes, they were.
question word + *(be)* + **subject** +			…?	Answers
Where	**was**	she	last year?	She was in England.

was not = wasn't,
were not = weren't

2   Grammar Check: *Asking and answering about vacation*
Write questions and answers. Use the words. Use past tense. (7 points)

1   you / be / on vacation last month? *Were you on vacation last month?*
    Yes, / I / go / to Sydney. *Yes,* _____

2   What / do / you / do / there? _____
    I / visit / my sister. _____

3   do / you / go / to the beach? _____
    Yes, / I / take / a surfing lesson _____

4   do / you / visit / the Opera House? _____
    No, I / have (not) / time. _____

3   Vocabulary Check: *What did you do last week?*
Complete the phrases. Change the verb to past tense. Then write the missing letters. (5 points)

1   (see)   I _*saw*_ a _m o v i e_.

2   (ride)   I _____ a _r_ _.

3   (have)   I _____ a _g_ _ _ _ _ _t_ _ _ _ _.

4   (take)   I _____ a _v_ _ _ _ _ _ _ _ _.

5   (give)   I _____ my grandmother a _h_ _ _ _.

6   (get)   I _____ a _p_ _ _ _ _ _ _ _ _.

Your score: _____ / 12

BONUS: You say a verb. Your partner says the verb in past tense.
     "eat"   *"ate"*

MIXER

1 → **TODAY'S GOAL:** Chat with 4 or more people

2 **Language Models** ◎ CD-2 **track 68** Listen and complete.

Excuse _me_, what did you do _l_ _ _ _ _v_ _ _ _ _ _ _ _ _?

Let _ _ see. I went to _D_ _ _ _ _ _ _ _ _ _.

Great, _w_ _h_ _ with?

_ _ _f_ _ _ _ _ _ _.

I see. _Wh_ _ _ did you _ _ in _ _ _ _ _ _ _ _ _ _ _ _?

I _t_ _ _ _k_ some pictures.

Anything else?

Yes, I went to the _b_ _ _ _ _. How about you?

3 **Think Time** What did your classmates do last vacation? Plan your questions.

1 _____

2 _____

3 _____

4 _____

IDEAS TO HELP YOU

- **worked**
- **played sports**
- **went camping**
- **went to a music festival**
- **had a barbecue**
- **enjoyed fireworks**
- **looked for a girlfriend/boyfriend!**

4 **Action** Stand up.
Chat to someone.
Check a box. ☑
Move. Chat to someone else.
Remember **TODAY'S GOAL!**

☐ 1st person
☐ 2nd person
☐ 3rd person
☐ 4th person

Even more people? ☐ ☐ ☐

5

How did I do?

☐ I did very well.
☐ I did well.
☐ I did OK.
☐ I had trouble.
☐ I had BIG trouble!

Now fill in the progress chart on page 121.

Solo *Was it a good weekend?*

1 Read about Paola, Roberto, and Bill. Fill in the blanks. There are two extra words.

all	rich	felt	romantic	~~enjoyed~~
spent	grandpa	free	great	before

This is Paola from Italy.

*Last weekend I had a date. I __enjoyed__ it. The dinner
was delicious and _____. Chatting was great. My
_____ is really interesting.*

This is Roberto from Brazil.

*I am _____ . This is a problem.
Last weekend I _____ too much money.
I bought presents for _____ my girlfriends.*

This is Bill from the U.S.

*I had a great weekend. I went to a pizza place with
a friend. I ate too many slices of pizza. I _____
sick. _____ day!*

2 CD-2 **tracks 69-71** Now listen. Check your answers.

On Your Own

- Extra Listening, page 128.
  Self-Study CD, tracks 76-83.
- Conversation. Listen and repeat.
  Self-Study CD, track 84.
- Solo. Listen and read. Self-Study CD, track 85.
- Language Check, Solo, Extra Practice
  www.efcafe.com.

3 **My writing:** How about **your** weekend?
Think about what you did. Write about it.

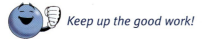

Keep up the good work!

unit 12 Will I be famous?

Preview

1 ◎ CD-2 **track 72** Listen. Point to the pictures.

be famous

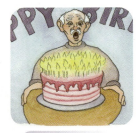

live a long life

get a good job

get an interesting job

work very hard

get a good grade

win a prize

get married

be rich

have many boyfriends

be on television

have many children

live in a different country

2 Listen again. Say the phrases.

3 Practice with a partner. Say five sentences about yourself.
Partner, do you agree?

I will be rich someday.   *I think you will!*
Really?
No way!

1 ⊙ CD-2 **tracks 73-77** Listen. Write the words:

will   am going to   is going to   are going to
won't   am not going to   is not going to   are not going to

2 I _____ study tonight.

1 It *will* _____ be sunny.

3 You _____ be famous someday.

4 She _____ live in Australia.

5 People _____ live in space soon.

2 Listen again. Are the speakers sure? Check (✓) your answers.

1 be sunny   ☐ **plan** ☐ **prediction**

2 study   ☐ **plan** ☐ **prediction**

3 be famous   ☐ **plan** ☐ **prediction**

4 live in another country   ☐ **plan** ☐ **prediction**

5 live in space   ☐ **plan** ☐ **prediction**

A **plan**: Something you will make happen. You are sure it will happen.

A **prediction**: Something you think will happen. Maybe you are wrong.

About You

⊙ CD-2 **track 78** Listen and answer.

1. _____

2. _____

3. _____

Compare answers with a partner.

1 CD-2 **track 79** Listen. Someone is learning about the future.

You will meet an interesting **woman**.

A **woman**? Will **she** be good-looking?

man   man   he he

Yes, very good-looking.

But **she** won't be rich.

Oh. What else?

She will be **American**.

American? Will I find true love?

He   **Canadian**   **Canadian**   him
Australian   **Australian**

Sorry. You're not going to love **her**. But you will learn a lot of English.

Oh.

2 Practice with a partner. Use the **blue** and **green** words.

3 Make your own conversation. Use your ideas.

Duet A *Your future*

Pronunciation ◉ **CD-2 track 80** Listen. Repeat silently. Then repeat out loud.

*Are you **go**ing to be **rich**?*	**Yes**, *I* **am**. / **Yes**, *I think* **so**. **No**, *I* **won't**.
*Will you **live** in a **di**fferent **ci**ty?*	**Yes**, *I* **will**. / **Yes**, *I think* **so**. **No**, *I* **won't**.

I'm sorry?

1 **Think Time** Read these questions. Which do you want to know about your future? Check (✓) at least 6 questions.

Am I going to… ☐ get a good job

☐ be famous someday?

☐ work very hard?

☐ win a prize?

☐ (one more – your idea):

Will I… ☐ have many boyfriends (or girlfriends)?

☐ have many children?

☐ live in a different city?

☐ become a very good English speaker?

☐ (one more – your idea):

2 Hold your arm straight. Hold a cell phone strap, keys, a necklace or a pencil by the top. It is about 6 centimeters (2 inches) over the "good luck." Close your eyes. Partner, ask the questions.
(*Are you…? Will you…?*)
Watch the pencil move. What does it say? Tell the answer.

3 Think of 3 more questions.

◗ **Challenge!**
Change partners. Ask more questions.
Look at page 106 for more ideas.

Duet B *Your future*

Pronunciation ◎ CD-2 **track 80** Listen. Repeat silently. Then repeat out loud.

Are you **go**ing to be **rich**?	**Yes**, I **am**. / **Yes**, I think **so**.
	No, I **won't**.
Will you **live** in a **diff**erent **city**?	**Yes**, I **will**. / **Yes**, I think **so**.
	No, I **won't**.

I'm sorry?

1 **Think Time** Read these questions. Which do you want to know about your future? Check (✓) at least 6 questions.

Am I going to...
- ☐ get a good job
- ☐ be famous someday?
- ☐ work very hard?
- ☐ win a prize?
- ☐ (one more – your idea):
_____

Will I...
- ☐ have many boyfriends (or girlfriends)?
- ☐ have many children?
- ☐ live in a different city?
- ☐ become a very good English speaker?
- ☐ (one more – your idea):
_____

2 Hold your arm straight. Hold a cell phone strap, keys, a necklace or a pencil by the top. It is about 6 centimeters (2 inches) over the "good luck." Close your eyes. Partner, ask the questions.
(Are you...? Will you...?)
Watch the pencil move. What does it say? Tell the answer.

3 Think of 3 more questions.

◯ **Challenge!**
Change partners. Ask more questions.
Look at page 106 for more ideas.

1   **Grammar Target:** "Will" and "going to" – "yes / no" questions

BE	+	subject	+	going to	verb	Answers
Are		**you**		*going to*	get married?	Yes, I am.
Is		**she**		*going to*	have many children?	No, she's not.

will	+	subject	+	verb	…?	Answers
Will		**they**		*live*	in a different country?	Yes, they will.
Will		**he**		*be*	famous?	No, he won't.

Positive Statements	Negative Statements
I'm going to get married.	I'm not going to get married.
She's going to have many children.	She's not going to have many children.
They'll live in a different country.	They won't live in a different country.
He'll be famous.	He won't be famous.

Remember:

won't = *will not*

I'll = *I will*

---

2   **Grammar Check:** *Talking about the future*

Fill in the correct word in each blank.   (6 points)

1   It __*is*__ going to rain this week.

2   He _____ be famous someday.

3   I _____ going to work hard next month.

4   She _____ going to live in New Zealand next year.

5   _____ you be rich someday?

6   _____ they going to get married?

7   They _____ have many children.

---

3   **Vocabulary Check:** *My dreams*   Fill in the blanks with a word or phrase.

There is one extra word.   (6 points)

long life	interesting job	girlfriends	famous	married	rich	children	~~on television~~

A: Someday I'll…   be __*on television*__. You will see me on Channel 7.

be _____. Everyone will know me.

be _____. I'll have a lot of money!

have many _____. All women will be in love with me.

B: I'm going to…   have an _____. Maybe I'll be a journalist.

get _____ . He will be a very good-looking man.

live a _____. I'll live to be 100 years old!

Your score: _____ / 12

BONUS: Work with a partner. Tell your partner your plans for the weekend. *"I'm going to …"*

Ensemble *I will be a great...*

MIXER

1 → **TODAY'S GOAL:** Chat with 4 or more people

2 **Language Models** 💿 CD-2 **track 81** Listen and complete.

In the future I w_ _ _ to be a d_ _ _o r.

I will g_ _ married and _ _ _ _ f_ _ _ children.

I will be a g_ _ _ _ f_ _ _ _ _!

_ _ the w_ _,

this weekend I'm _ _ _ _ _ to our sc_ _ _ _ _ festival.

I'm going to _ _ _ _ soup

and _ _ _ _ it _ _ the festival.

H_ _ about you?

3 **Think Time** What will your classmates be? What will they do? Plan your questions.

1 _____

2 _____

3 _____

4 _____

IDEAS TO HELP YOU

- kind
- fair
- strict
- loving
- wonderful
- super
- successful
- bad
- terrible

4 **Action** Stand up.
Chat to someone.

Check a box. ☑
Move. Chat to someone else.

Remember **TODAY'S GOAL!**

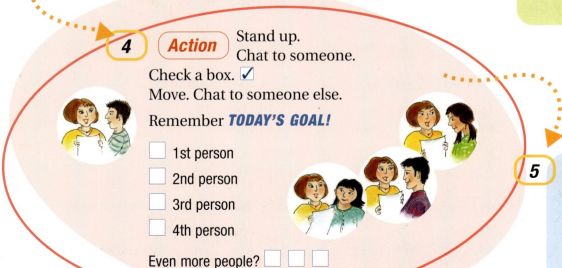

- [ ] 1st person
- [ ] 2nd person
- [ ] 3rd person
- [ ] 4th person

Even more people? [ ] [ ] [ ]

5 **How did I do?**

- [ ] I did very well.
- [ ] I did well.
- [ ] I did OK.
- [ ] I had trouble.
- [ ] I had BIG trouble!

Now fill in the progress chart on page 121.

1 Read about these people's predictions. Fill in the blanks. There are two extra words.

~~super~~   national   healthy   enjoy   more

stronger   together   using   great   between   popular

This is Mike from the U.S.

In the future I think China will be the next world ___super___ power and Americans will worry about it. NBA players will be _____ than 270 cm tall. I'll get married. My partner and I will have two _____ children.

This is Ana from Brazil.

In the future I think Brazilian culture will become more _____ around the world. More people will listen to Brazilian music. Of course, our _____ soccer team will win the next World Cup. I will marry a famous Brazilian soccer player.

This is Kyong Suk from Korea.

In the future I think the friendship _____ Korean and Japanese people will become stronger and stronger. Also I hope the leaders of Japan and Korea can share ideas and work _____ well. I will study English at university.

This is Bahar from Turkey.

In the future I think Turkey will become _____ in Europe. Companies in Turkey will grow quickly. I will find a great job _____ English in business.

2 CD-2 **tracks 82-85**   Now listen. Check your answers.

3 **My writing:** What are **your** ideas about the future? Think about them. Write about them.

 Congratulations! You did it! You have a great future in English!

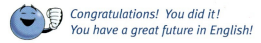 **On Your Own**

- Extra Listening, page 129. Self-Study CD, tracks 86-90.
- Conversation. Listen and repeat. Self-Study CD, track 91.
- Solo. Listen and read. Self-Study CD, track 92.
- Language Check, Solo, Extra Practice www.efcafe.com.

113

1 Work with a partner.
Choose a word. Think of a sentence with that word. Say the sentence.
Don't say the word. Say BLANK.
Partner, guess the word. Count your partner's guesses.

Check (✔) your partner's guesses.

☐☐☐☐☐ ☐☐☐☐☐
☐☐☐☐☐ ☐☐☐☐☐
☐☐☐☐☐ ☐☐☐☐☐
☐☐☐☐☐ ☐☐☐☐☐
☐☐☐☐☐ ☐☐☐☐☐

My favorite sport is BLANK.

Bowling? Soccer?

prize (page 110)

between (94)

went (102)

peppers (74)

soccer (85)

bowling (85)

different (110)

hanging out (84)

rice (79)

bathtub (90)

sandwich (74)

play (71)

studied (98)

always (71)

weekend (70)

closet (92)

hardly ever (71)

mangoes (79)

visit (102)

interesting (111)

vacation (103)

surf the internet (69)

swimming (82)

practicing (86)

boyfriend / girlfriend (110)

fridge (91)

salsa (75)

journalist (111)

ate (99)

beans (74)

watch (102)

clean (72)

plant (95)

basketball (82)

You will review *English Firsthand Access*, Units 7–12 and Unit Zero.

Unit Zero

Work with **B**. Do you remember these sentences?

How do you spell it?
W____ ___ ___ m____?
W____ (_____) ___ E_____?
P_____?
E_____ ___?
I___ _____?

Unit 7: I love weekends!

1 Say one sentence about yourself for each word.
always   usually   sometimes   hardly ever   never

2 Listen to **B**. Say:
Me, too.
Me, either.
Not me, I (always, usually, etc) *do.*

Unit 8: Do you have any onions?

You and **B** are going on a picnic. Take something that starts with every letter of the alphabet (A-Z, except X). Say what you will bring:

You: *We need some apples.*
Do we have any bananas?

B: *No, we need some bananas.*
Do we have any carrots? ...

Unit 9: What are they doing?

How many different things are you doing right now? With **B**, say them.
We're speaking English. We're sitting in chairs.
Make one check (✓) for each **-ing** word.

☐☐☐☐☐ ☐☐☐☐☐
☐☐☐☐☐ ☐☐☐☐☐

Unit 10: My house is not so big

1 Describe your picture. **B** will draw.
2 Listen. Draw **B**'s picture.

Unit 11: Where did you go?

1 Think of a very good time in your life. What did you do? Tell **B**.
I was...   I went...   I saw...
Make one check (✓) for every past tense verb.
☐☐☐☐☐☐☐☐☐

2 Listen to **B**. Ask questions.

Unit 12: Will I be famous?

1 What are your plans and dreams? Finish these sentences:
This year I'm going to...
In five years, I'll...
In 10 years, I'll...
Someday, I'll...

2 Listen. Ask questions.
Make comments (*Great. Wow. Cool,* etc.)

You're using English, firsthand.

You've got ACCESS!

You're heading for SUCCESS!

115

You will review *English Firsthand Access*, Units 7–12 and Unit Zero.

Unit Zero

Work with **A**. Do you remember these sentences?

How do you spell it ?
W___ ___ ____ m____?
W____ (____) __ E_____?
P_____?
E_____ ___?
I__ _____?

Unit 7: I love weekends!

1 Listen to **A**. Say:
   Me, too.
   Me, either.
   Not me, I (always, usually, etc) *do.*

2 Say one sentence about yourself for each word.
   always   usually   sometimes   hardly ever   never

Unit 8: Do you have any onions?

You and **A** are going on a picnic. Take something that starts with every letter of the alphabet (A-Z, except X). Say what you will bring:

A: *We need some **apples**.*
      *Do we have any **bananas**?*

You: *No, we need some **bananas**.*
       *Do we have any **carrots**? ...*

Unit 9: What are they doing?

How many different things are you doing right now? With **A**, say them.
   *We're **speaking** English. We're **sitting** in chairs.*
Make one check (✓) for each **-ing** word.

☐☐☐☐☐ ☐☐☐☐☐
☐☐☐☐☐ ☐☐☐☐☐

Unit 10: My house is not so big

1 Listen. Draw **A**'s picture.
2 Describe your picture. **A** will draw.

Unit 11: Where did you go?

2 Listen to **A**. Ask questions.
1 Think of a very good time in your life. What did you do? Tell **A**.
   I was...   I went...   I saw...
   Make one check (✓) for every past tense verb.
   ☐☐☐☐☐☐☐☐☐☐

Unit 12: Will I be famous?

1 Listen. Ask questions.
   Make comments (*Great. Wow. Cool*, etc.)
2 What are your plans and dreams? Finish these sentences:
   This year I'm going to...
   In five years, I'll...
   In 10 years, I'll...
   Someday, I'll...

You're using English, firsthand.   *You've got ACCESS!*

You're heading for SUCCESS!

116

Let's Talk: *A conversation game*

This is a speaking game. Work in groups of 3 or 4.

1 **Think Time** Look at the questions. Which are interesting? Decide on 5 (or more) to answer. Circle them. What will you say? Think about your answers.

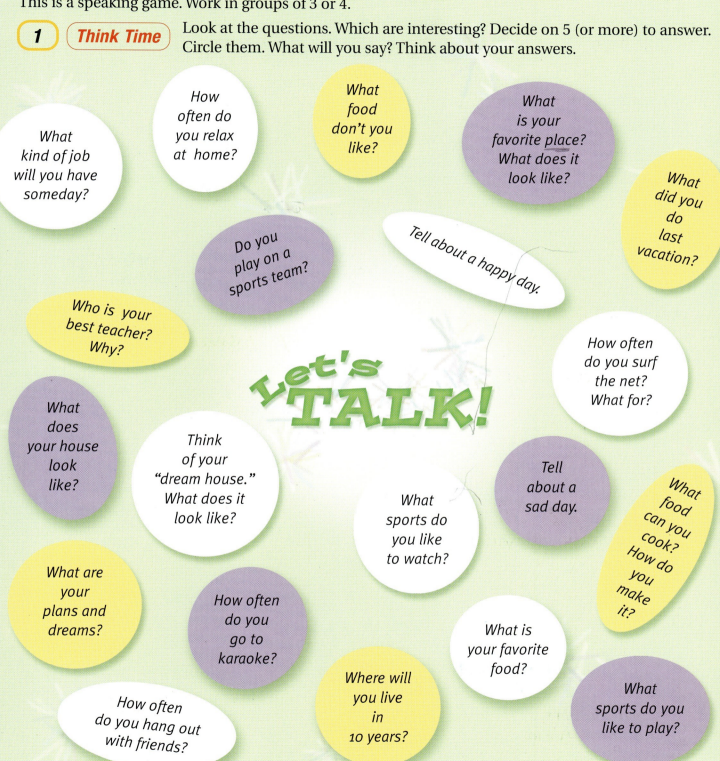

What kind of job will you have someday?

How often do you relax at home?

What food don't you like?

What is your favorite place? What does it look like?

What did you do last vacation?

Do you play on a sports team?

Tell about a happy day.

Who is your best teacher? Why?

How often do you surf the net? What for?

What does your house look like?

Think of your "dream house." What does it look like?

What sports do you like to watch?

Tell about a sad day.

What food can you cook? How do you make it?

What are your plans and dreams?

How often do you go to karaoke?

What is your favorite food?

What sports do you like to play?

How often do you hang out with friends?

Where will you live in 10 years?

2 Play the game. Put a space marker on a question. Answer it. Give long answers. Partners, ask questions. Take turns. Enjoy your conversation.

		Do you have any tomatoes?	Do you have any potato chips?
1 package		Do you have any mustard?	Do you have any hot dog buns?
a few	3 bags	Do you have any peppers?	Do you have any chicken?
10 ears	a lot	Do you have any ice tea?	Do you have any mushrooms?
a little		Do you have any salad?	Do you have any onions?
1 bottle		Do you have any barbecue sauce?	Do you have any corn?
2 liters	about 12	Do you have any mangoes?	Do you have any ice?
1 case - 24 cans	a lot	Do you have any drinks?	Do you have any ice cream?
1 package	2 liters	Do you have any sausages?	Do you have any beans?

120

Ensemble Progress Chart

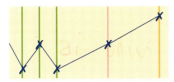

Look at "How did I do?" on the Ensemble page.
Mark an ✗ on this chart. Join your ✗s. Can you see your progress?

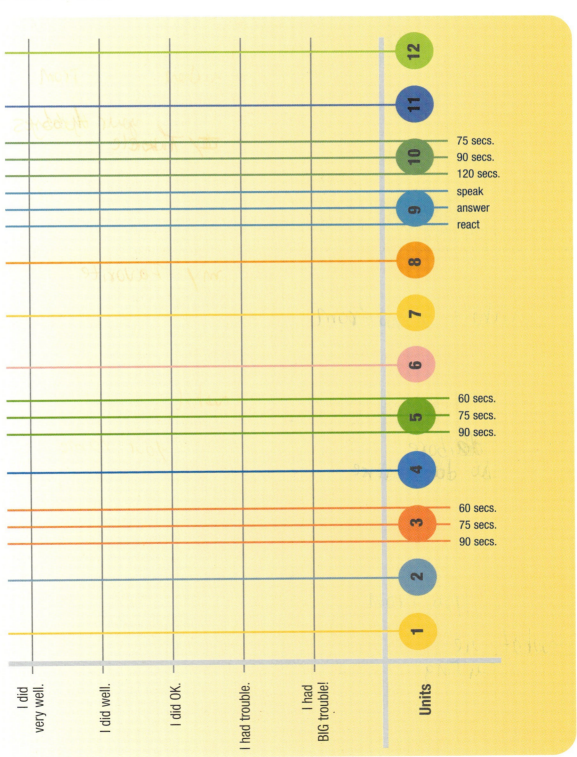

Extra Listening

Unit 0

Self-Study CD **track 2**

1 _____ do you spell it?
2 What does (that) _my_ ?
3 _what_ (that) in English?
4 _____ ?
5 I'm _sorry_ ?
6 _skims_ me?

Unit 1

1. Self-Study CD **track 3**

I Hello. Your name is…
K Kanjana.
I Kanjana?
K Yes. K-A-N-J-A-N-A.
I OK. _where are you From_ from, Kanjana?
K Bangkok. Bangkok, Thailand.
I I see. Kanjana, what are your hobbies?
K Hobbies? I like dancing.
I Dancing?
K Yeah, my _Talbove_ thing is dancing.
I OK. So _so do yo like_ music?
K Yeah. Pop. I like pop music.

2. Self-Study CD **track 4**

I Hi, Eric. How are you doing?
E Good.
I Where are _you From_ , Eric?
E Canada. I'm from Toronto, Canada.
I _what are_ your hobbies?
E Hmm. _Surfing_ the internet.
I Surfing the internet.
E Right. I spend a lot of time on the internet.

I How about music. _who is_ your favorite singer?
E Diddy. I love hip-hop.

3. Self-Study CD **track 5**

I _where_ are you _From_ , Ming?
M Taipei. Taipei, Taiwan.
I What are _your Hobbies_ ?
M _I like_ sports. Especially swimming.
I You like swimming?
M Oh, yes, I really like it.
I Anything else?
M I like reading. Love stories are _my Favorite_.
I OK, that's interesting.

Unit 2

1. Self-Study CD **track 8**

A _what_ your name.
B Pardon?
A Write _your name_. Here. On the line.
B Oh. OK.

2. Self-Study CD **track 9**

A When is your birthday? Write it on the line.
B _____ _____?
A When is your birthday? When were you born? _____ _____ on the line.
B Right.

3. Self-Study CD **track 10**

A Check B.
B _____ _____ _____ "B" or "V"?

Extra Listening

A _____ B. You know: A - "B" - C

B Oh. B? I see

4. Self-Study CD **track 11**

A _____ 16.

B _____ _____ ?

A Circle 16: one - six.

B Circle 16: one - six.

5. Self-Study CD **track 12**

A Draw a house.

B _____ does that _____ ?

A A house. The place you live. _____
_____ _____ / of a house / the
place you live.

B Ah. House.

6. Self-Study CD **track 13**

A _____ _____ .

B _____ do you _____ it?

A House: H-O-U-S-E

B H-O-U-S-E.

Unit 3

1. Self-Study CD **track 16**

What do I have in my bag? It's full of lots
of stuff. Let me see. _____ _____ two
books. An English textbook and a math
book. What else? Oh, a dictionary. For
English class. There are one, two, three
pens. All the pens are blue. There are …
No, there's one pencil. Oh! And my _____
_____ , of course. I love listening
to music.

2. Self-Study CD **track 17**

_____ _____ my bag for work. I have
another bag for sports. Right now,
_____ _____ too much in my bag.
Most of my stuff is on my desk at the
office. Here, _____ _____ a few folders, my _____ , a pen, and some lipstick. Not too much. But I'm a hard worker… really!

3. Self-Study CD **track 18**

This bag is so heavy. Why did I put so
much stuff in here? I have my snacks and
_____ _____ . I have a _____ .
I take a lot of pictures. And it's a sunny
day, so I have _____ _____ .

4. Self-Study CD **track 19**

_____ _____ my everyday bag. I have my
_____ and a book in here. I like to
read on the train. I also have some snacks
for my son. And some gum, too. _____
_____ there's room for in the bag.

Unit 4

1. Self-Study CD **track 22**

I _____ _____ at nine o'clock. Nine
every morning. I work _____ five-thirty. I finish at five-thirty in the afternoon.

2. Self-Study CD **track 23**

I study _____ _____ . Some people
wait till Sunday, but I study a little every
day. I study _____ dinner, from 7:30
to about nine.

3. Self-Study CD **track 24**

I love to exercise. I _____ _____ four times a week. I work out at the same time. I always work out at four o'clock. I finish at _____ five-fifteen.

4. Self-Study CD **track 25**

_____ _____ do I wake up? The same time every day. Six o'clock. I like to _____ ____ early. It's so beautiful at six.

5. Self-Study CD **track 26**

_____ I do my homework, I _____ chat a little with friends online. We text each other all day, but we like to chat too, when we get home. I guess I chat for about an hour, from eight to nine.

6. Self-Study CD **track 27**

It's time for me to go to bed. I'm tired. I go to bed _____, at ten. I go to bed _____ _____, and then I get up early.

Unit 5

1. Self-Study CD **track 30**

This is my family. My father is very _____. My mother? She's _____. She is always busy doing something. I have one older brother and one _____ _____. They are very different. My brother is shy, but my sister is _____. She has a lot of friends.

2. Self-Study CD **track 31**

My family? Well, my father is _____

_____. He exercises a lot and doesn't eat any junk food. My mother is _____. She looks very young. My grandmother lives with us, too. She is _____ _____. She tells funny stories. She always makes me laugh. I have a twin sister. She's very _____. We're exactly alike!

3. Self-Study CD **track 32**

I have a small family. My father is _____. He likes to tell jokes. My mother is _____ _____. She reads a lot. I don't have any brothers or sisters. I'm an only child. But we have two pets. A very _____ cat and a _____ dog.

Unit 6

1. Self-Study CD **track 35**

A Tell me about your favorite clothes.

B Hmm. My favorite clothes. I have a really cool _____ _____ _____. They're _____ _____. Black and red. I love them.

2. Self-Study CD **track 36**

A Tell me about your favorite clothes.

B I have a summer _____ I really like. It has a _____ _____ – big yellow sunflowers. It's really pretty.

3. Self-Study CD **track 37**

A _____ _____ of clothes do you like?

B My favorite clothes in the summer are shorts. White, cotton shorts. They feel _____.

Extra Listening

4. Self-Study CD **track 38**

A What are your favorite clothes?

B I've got a leather jacket I like a lot. It was a present. It's a designer brand, so it was probably _____, but it is really _____.

5. Self-Study CD **track 39**

A Tell me about the clothes you like the most.

B I have a really stylish sweater. It's from Australia. It is made of wool so it is warm. It has really _____ _____ — red and blue and yellow.

6. Self-Study CD **track 40**

A What are your favorite clothes?

B Just jeans, I guess. Just plain blue jeans. They are _____ and _____.

Unit 7

1. Self-Study CD **track 43**

I Hi, Kate. How is your band?

K Great! We sound really good.

I _____ _____ do you have band practice?

K Oh, very often. We practice _____ _____.

I How often do you give concerts?

K Concerts? _____ _____. We only have a few songs.

I How often do you sing in the band?

K Me? ____ _____ sing. I play drums.

2. Self-Study CD **track 44**

I Hi, Koji.

K Hey!

I _____ ____ _____ do on weekends?

K I always _____ _____ with my friends.

I How often do you go to the movies?

K Mm, movies? Hardly ever.

I How about karaoke? _____ _____ _____ to karaoke?

K Um, _____. My friends and I go from time to time.

3. Self-Study CD **track 45**

I Hi, Manee. What do you _____ do on weekends?

M Well, for me, the weekend means "relax." I _____ _____ _____ on Saturday morning.

I How often do you go shopping?

M Sometimes I go on Sunday afternoon. I love to buy clothes.

I How about studying? How often do you study?

M I _____ _____ on Sunday evening. I'm a _____ student.

Unit 8

1. Self-Study CD **track 48**

A We'll want to make _____.

B Yeah, sandwiches.

A So _____ _____ _____.

B Right. Which do you like, white or wheat?

A Wheat. How about the light brown one?

B Is one _____ enough?

A One loaf? Yeah, that's fine.

2. Self-Study CD **track 49**

A We're going to make _____ pizza, right? So we'll need some of these.

B Yeah. These look good. Bright red color. The red ones are ready to cook.

A _____ _____?

B Maybe 5. Yeah, five should be _____.

3. Self-Study CD **track 50**

A Mmmmm. Smell this.

B Oh, that smells great. Really strong.

A Yeah, I love it in the morning.

B Yeah. How much?

A 500 _____.

B 500 grams. Good.

4. Self-Study CD **track 51**

A Do we need any…?

B Yeah. Um, one _____?

A Yeah, one carton should do it. Oh, be careful!

B Oops.

A Nice catch.

B _____ scrambled them right here.

5. Self-Study CD **track 52**

A You want the hot or the medium?

B I like really _____. That OK with you?

A Oh yeah. I love hot stuff.

B One bottle?

A Maybe _____ _____. We don't want to run out.

B Two bottles it is.

6. Self-Study CD **track 53**

A Hmm. These are all kind of green.

B Look over there. There are some yellow ones.

A OK, yeah, these are ripe. They're yellow.

B _____ _____ _____ here? 5-6-7-8. Eight. Is that OK?

A Yeah, 8's good.

Unit 9

1. Self-Study CD **track 56**

A Look at this picture. Isn't it great?

B Who's that?

A It's my grandmother. She's _____ _____. She loves to play tennis.

B Play tennis? That's great!

A Yeah, she's really good, too.

2. Self-Study CD **track 57**

A Where's your brother?

B _____ _____ the computer.

A Is he still on the computer? I told him just another half hour.

B He's still online.

A Sean!

3. Self-Study CD **track 58**

A What's this picture on your website?

B That's my birthday party. That's _____ _____ _____ "Happy Birthday" to me.

A Does she have a good voice?

Extra Listening

B Really good. She wants to be a professional singer.

4.

A Hello?

B Hi! What are _____ _____?

A _____ _____. Can I call you back?

B Eating? It's late!

A I just got home. I'm so hungry. Call you back.

5.

A Want to see some video? This is great.

B Sure. Hey, what's that guy doing?

A Skydiving. That's my brother. _____ _____.

B He's _____!

6.

A Where's your grandfather?

B _____ _____ _____.

A Hanging out? I _____ _____ grandfathers hang out.

B I don't know. He looks like he's hanging out.

7.

A Where's your father?

B _____ _____ basketball with the neighbors.

A Playing basketball?

B Yeah, _____ _____ _____ a long time.

8.

A Have you seen your mother?

B: _____ _____.

A Reading? Where is she?

B: She's upstairs.

Unit 10

1.

A Could you help me put the dishes _____ the table?

B Sure. Uh, where do you keep them?

A Oh, they're _____ _____ _____, in the cupboard over the stove, _____ shelf.

B Oh, I see them.

2.

B And the glasses? Do you want me to put glasses on the _____, too?

A Yeah, the ones in the cupboard, _____ _____ _____ _____, left.

B On the left of the top shelf?

A Yes, please.

3.

A Would you get some juice, too? It's _____ _____ _____, top shelf. On the right, I think.

B Yeah, here it is, _____ _____ _____.

4.

B Oh, I forgot the forks and spoons.

A Forks and spoons are in the drawer next to the sink.

B _____ _____ _____ _____? Oh, here they are.

Extra Listening

5. Self-Study CD **track 70**

B I have to make a phone call. What time is it?

A I can't see, but there's a clock _____

_____ _____.

B Ah, not time yet. I'll call later.

6. Self-Study CD **track 71**

C Mom, where's my bag?

A It's _____ _____ _____, where you left it.

C Oops. Sorry.

7. Self-Study CD **track 72**

A Hey, put your glass in the sink.

C _____ _____ _____. It is!

A That's news.

8. Self-Study CD **track 73**

A OK. We're ready. Let's have a cup of tea.

B I made _____. It's on the stove.

A Oh, thanks. You've been a big help!

Unit 11

1. Self-Study CD **track 76**

A What did you do last night?

B I _____ _____. I watched old movies all night.

A Oh, really? What did you watch?

B I watched "Casablanca," and…

A Oh, I love that movie!

2. Self-Study CD **track 77**

A What did you do last weekend?

B Last weekend? I _____ _____. I

went shopping and spent too much money. I spent way too much money.

A How much did you spend?

B Oh, **too** much, _____ _____

_____ to know…

3. Self-Study CD **track 78**

A _____ _____ _____ ____

on your vacation?

B I went to New York City.

A Really? For how long?

B I _____ _____ for a week.

A Cool. Did you like it?

B Loved it. I want to go back right now!

4. Self-Study CD **track 79**

A Is that a new sweater?

B Yeah, I got it for my birthday. It _____

_____ _____ from my mom.

A You know, green is a great color for you.

B Thanks.

5. Self-Study CD **track 80**

A What did you do last weekend?

B A friend and I _____ _____ ____

_____. We ate at a Chinese restaurant.

A Yeah? Was it any good?

B Incredible food. Just great. You should check it out.

A Where is it?

B It's a new place across from… across from the subway station…

6. Self-Study CD **track 81**

A _____ _____ _____ a good

time on your vacation?

B _____ _____ a really good time. I went to the beach.

A Oh, I'd love to go to the beach. It's been so cold here.

B Yeah, I miss it already.

7. Self-Study CD **track 82**

A What did you do last weekend?

B I was busy. I studied for a test.

A Yeah? What kind of test.

B Oh, a big history test. I _____ _____ _____. I think I _____ _____ on it.

8. Self-Study CD **track 83**

A Where's your car?

B I _____ the bus today.

A Is something wrong with your car?

B No, I just get tired of driving in all the traffic. That's all.

Unit 12

1. Self-Study CD **track 86**

A Tomorrow's weather _____ _____ _____. The sun will be shining all day tomorrow.

2. Self-Study CD **track 87**

A We're _____ _____ after school.

B Where?

A Downtown. _____ _____ _____ to come?

B Oh, gee, I can't. I'm _____ _____. I'm going to study tonight. Big test _____.

3. Self-Study CD **track 88**

A Wow. That is so good. Play some more. Yes, that's really good… _____ _____ _____. I just know it. You'll be famous someday.

4. Self-Study CD **track 89**

A Did you hear about Mi Soon?

B No, what?

A Her family is moving to Australia.

B Really? Australia?

A Yes! She's _____ _____ _____ in Sydney for two years.

B She's going to live in Australia? Cool.

A Yeah, she's _____!

5. Self-Study CD **track 90**

A And we're talking to space scientist Brian O. Miles. Good afternoon, Dr. Miles.

B Good afternoon.

A Tell us, _____ _____ _____ _____ in space anytime soon?

B A few people, yes. A lot of people? No.

A You don't think so?

B No, that's _____ _____ to happen. Large numbers of people _____ _____ in space soon. _____ _____ to send astronauts to the space station, but people won't live in space soon.

A Well, … Do you think …

Vocabulary Maps

Here are lists of important vocabulary from each unit. Use these lists to review the words from each unit. There are also **more words** to expand your vocabulary.

You'll also find some common "collocations." These are words that often go together.

Unit 0
Keywords

Likes

listening to
practicing
reading
sleeping
writing
talking
dogs
blue
green

more words
going
living
watching
working
playing
spell
mean
say

Understanding

spell
mean
say

more words
repeat

Vocabulary Maps

Unit 1
Keywords

Music

pop (popular)
classical
hip-hop
rock

more words
modern
live
black
traditional
jazz
blues
world
latin

Sports

soccer
tennis
swimming

more words
football
baseball
basketball
running
golf

Books and movies

adventures
love stories
comics

more words
action
business
horror
historical movies
comedies
popular
modern
old

Other interests

reading
eating
talking
shopping
dancing
playing video games
the internet

more words
sleeping
going out
cooking
learning
studying
relaxing
cars
travel
drinking

Collocations

Actor

best
good
young
famous
great
new
my favorite
one of my
   favorite(s)

Singer

new
good
young
American
famous
best
my favorite
one of my
   favorite(s)

Favorite

food
place
subject
pastime
game
spot
color
music
song
restaurant
TV show
word
story
movie

Vocabulary Maps

Unit 2
Keywords

Directives

find
write
check
cross out
say
point to
touch
draw
take

more words

look
try to
let's
come
listen
put
give
tell
move
wait

Days

Monday
Tuesday
Wednesday
Thursday
Friday
Saturday
Sunday
yesterday
today
tomorrow

Months

January
February
March
April
May
June
July
August
September
October
November
December

Unit 3
Keywords

In a room

desk
chair
computer
printer
shelf
floor
table

more words

bed
pictures
door
carpet
bookcase
corner
piano

In a bag

dictionary
notebook
paper
pen
pencil
MP3 player
bottled water
camera
lipstick
money

more words

stuff

Collocations

Room prepositions

on / by / behind
    the door
on the table
on / in the desk
under the lamp
on / under the carpet
on / in the bookcase
in the corner
in front of the TV

Room

dark
ground-floor
front
single
warm
empty
comfortable
tiny
small
large
cold

Vocabulary Maps

Unit 4
Keywords

Activity verbs

word
study
listen (to)
watch
practice
do homework
listening
read

more words

make
get
go
give
take
come
use
leave
show
try
buy
move
follow

Time adverbs

now
then
today
every
how
again

more words

always
still
never
ago
ever
just
yesterday
already
sometimes
often
usually

Other time words

day
night
when
breakfast
time
early
dinner
Sunday
Saturday
late
morning

Other interests

reading
eating
talking
shopping
dancing
playing video games
the internet

more words

sleeping
going out
cooking
learning
studying
relaxing
cars
travel
drinking

Collocations

Time prepositions

on / during + day
at / on + night
for / at + breakfast
at / for / by /
   during + time

Work

do
get
go
make
find

Homework

do
have

Listen (to)

music
radio
people

Watch

TV
time
space
video
people

Vocabulary Maps

Unit 5
Keywords

Describing people

quiet
friendly
hardworking
happy
serious
healthy
intelligent

more words

nice
young
elderly
single
disabled
different
dead
married

Family & friends

sister
brother
mother / mom
father / dad
partner
grandmother
grandfather

more words

husband
wife
son
daughter

Jobs

musician
singer

more words

manager
doctor
teacher
driver
worker
guard

Unit 6
Keywords

Colors

blue
black
white
red
green
brown
gray
yellow

Fashion nouns

clothes
bag
clothing
designer
jacket
cotton
shoes
dress
shirt
belt
brand

Adjectives

flowered
great
short
small
large
new
cool
solid
pretty
bright
comfortable
cheap
expensive

Shopping nouns

shop
item
shopper
price
money
seller
service
sale

Shopping verbs

buy
sell
cost
shop

Vocabulary Maps

Unit 7
Keywords

Activities	**Interests**	**Frequency adverbs**
listen	sports	always
write	TV	(not) usually
play	dancing	(not) often
watch	music	sometimes
work	movies	never
practice	games	
read	video	
study	art	
chat	concerts	
cook	internet	

Collocations

Go + -ing

shopping

more words
swimming
fishing

Unit 8
Keywords

Food adjectives	**Food & drink**	**Containers**
hot	water	bag
sweet	tea	package
spicy	eggs	bottle
	bread	can
more words	fish	
fresh	milk	
different	ice	
local	chicken	
healthy	cream	
excellent	coffee	
natural	meal	
fried	meat	
	fruit	
	vegetables	

Collocations

bottle of wine
bottle of beer
glass of water
cup of tea
piece of bread
cup of coffee
piece of meat
piece of fruit

Vocabulary Maps

Unit 9
Keywords

Activities

making	listening
running	singing
talking	swimming
playing	dancing
watching	jumping
speaking	snowboarding
fighting	

Collocations

Making

decisions
money
progress
effort

Running

down
out
up
away
around

Talking

to
about

Unit 10
Keywords

House

room
home
bedroom
kitchen
bathroom
apartment
toilet

Objects

table
picture
glasses
book
boxes
bed
chair
dishes

Other places

country
area
England
middle
location
Canada

Prepositions of place

in
on
under
at
over
between
behind
by

Collocations

at home
in the house
in the room
by the house
around the room
outside the home
inside the house

Vocabulary Maps

Unit 11
Keywords

Past tense verbs

made	spent
went	played
got	bought
took	watched
felt	
saw	**more words**
gave	said
tried	came
looked	thought
worked	knew

Collocations

Made

a mistake
me laugh
me feel…

Went

to the doctor
to see…
into the apartment

Got

a lot
a job
a letter

Took

the lead
it to the…

Felt

that…
like saying…

Unit 12
Keywords

Will + verbs

get
see
say
make
know
find
tell
become
look
want

(be) going to + verbs

get
say
go
put

more words
happen
give
take
let

Won't + verbs

get	take
go	come
say	let
know	give
see	need

Collocations

Get the chance…
Get better
Get married
Make sure
Become clear

Months & Numbers

Days of the week

Sunday, Monday, Tuesday, Wednesday, Thursday, Friday, Saturday

Months of the year

Numbers

1	2	3	4	5	6	7	8	9	10
one	two	three	four	five	six	seven	eight	nine	ten

11	12	13	14	15	16	17	18	19	20
eleven	twelve	thirteen	fourteen	fifteen	sixteen	seventeen	eighteen	nineteen	twenty

21	22	23	24	25	26	27	28	29	30
twenty-one	twenty-two	twenty-three	twenty-four	twenty-five	twenty-six	twenty-seven	twenty-eight	twenty-nine	thirty

40	50	60	70	80	90	100
forty	fifty	sixty	seventy	eighty	ninety	one hundred

1,000	10,000	1,000,000
one thousand	ten thousand	one million

Counting Numbers (Ordinals)

1st	2nd	3rd	4th	5th	6th	7th	8th	9th	10th
first	second	third	fourth	fifth	sixth	seventh	eighth	ninth	tenth

11th	12th	13th	14th	15th	16th	17th	18th	19th	20th
eleventh	twelfth	thirteenth	fourteenth	fifteenth	sixteenth	seventeenth	eighteenth	nineteenth	twentieth

21st	22nd	23rd	24th	25th	26th	27th	28th	29th	30th
twenty-first	twenty-second	twenty-third	twenty-fourth	twenty-fifth	twenty-sixth	twenty-seventh	twenty-eighth	twenty-ninth	thirtieth

31st...	100th...	1,000th ...	10,000th ...	1,000,000th
thirty-first	one-hundredth	one-thousandth	one-ten-thousandth	one-millionth

Countries & Nationalities

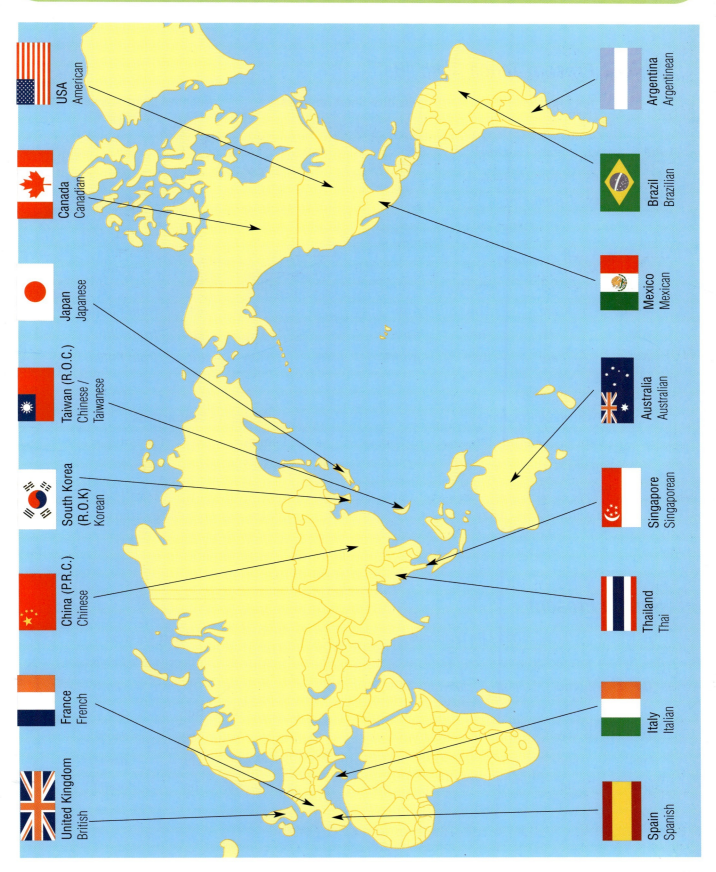

USA
American

Canada
Canadian

Japan
Japanese

Taiwan (R.O.C.)
Chinese /
Taiwanese

South Korea
(R.O.K)
Korean

China (P.R.C.)
Chinese

France
French

United Kingdom
British

Argentina
Argentinean

Brazil
Brazilian

Mexico
Mexican

Australia
Australian

Singapore
Singaporean

Thailand
Thai

Italy
Italian

Spain
Spanish

Grammar Charts

Simple Present Tense *Verb "Be"*

Yes / No Questions			Positive Short Answers			Negative Short Answers			
Be + subject... ?			subject + **be**			subject + **be** + not			
Are	you	*from Canada?*	Yes,	I	**am**.	No,	I	**am**	not.
Is	he	*from China?*		he	**is**.		he	**is**	not.
Are	they	*from Korea?*		they	**are**.		they	**are**	not.

WH- Questions				Answers			
question word + **(be)** + subject + ...?				Subject + **be**			
Where	**are**	you	*from?*	I	**am**	*from Canada.*	
Where	**is**	he	*from?*	He	**is**	*from China.*	
Where	**are**	they	*from?*	They	**are**	*from Korea.*	

Positive Contractions			Negative Contractions		
I am	=	I'm	I am not	=	I'm not
You are	=	You're	You are not	=	You aren't
We are	=	We're	We are not	=	We aren't
They are	=	They're	They are not	=	They aren't

Simple Present

Yes / No Questions				Short Answers			
Do / Does + subject + *verb* + ?				subject + **do / does** (**not**)			
Do	you	*finish*	*class at 2:30 on Mondays?*	Yes,	I	**do**.	
Do	they			No,	they	**don't**.	
Do	we			No,	we	**don't**.	
Does	she	*eat*	*breakfast every morning?*	Yes,	she	**does**.	
Does	he			No,	he	**doesn't**.	

Grammar Charts

Simple Present, continued

WH- Questions				Answers		
question word + *do/does* + subject + *verb*?				Subject + *verb*		
What	**do**	you	*like to do?*	I	*like*	*dancing.*
Where	**do**	they	*live?*	They	*live*	*in Taiwan.*
When	**do**	we	*start class?*	We	*start*	*class at 10:00.*
What	**does**	he	*like to do?*	He	*likes*	*snowboarding.*
Where	**does**	she	*live?*	She	*lives*	*in Chicago.*
When	**does**	it (this class)	*start?*	It	*starts*	*at 10:00.*

Contractions with "Do"			
I / you / we / they	**do** not	I / you / we / they	**don't**
He / She / It	**does** not	He / She / It	**doesn't**

Present Continuous

Yes / No Questions				Short Answers		
Be + subject + *verb* + *ing* ?				subject + *verb*		
Is	he	*play*ing	*soccer?*	*Yes,*	he	*is.*
Are	you	*watch*ing	*TV?*	*No,*	I *'m*	not.
Are	they	*do*ing	*homework?*	*Yes,*	they	*are.*

WH- Questions				Answers			
question word + *(be)* + subject + *verb* + *ing*?				Subject + *be* + *verb* + *ing*			
What	**are**	you	*do*ing?	I'	*m*	*eat*ing	*lunch.*
Where	**are**	they	*watch*ing?	They'	*re*	*watch*ing	*TV.*
What	**is**	she	*eat*ing?	She'	*s*	*eat*ing	*pizza.*

Grammar Charts

Simple Past Verb "Be"

Yes / No Questions			Short Answers		
Was / Were + subject		...?	subject + **was / were** (**not**)		
Was	he	on vacation last week?	Yes,	he	**was**.
Was	she	in class yesterday?	No,	she	**wasn't**.
Was	it	a nice hotel?	No,	it	**wasn't**.
Were	you	in Tokyo last weekend?	Yes,	I	**was**.
Were	they	at the beach yesterday?	No,	they	**weren't**.

Simple Past

Yes / No Questions				Short Answers		
Did + subject + **verb**			...?	subject + **did** (**not**)		
Did	you	go	to Australia last year?	Yes,	I	**did**.
Did	she	go	to Australia last year?	No,	she	**didn't**.
Did	they	go	to Australia last year?	Yes,	they	**did**.

WH- Questions				Answers		
question word + **did** + subject + **verb**?				Subject + **verb**		
Where	**did**	you	**go**?	I	**went**	to Sydney.
Who	**did**	she	**visit**?	She	**visited**	her cousins.
What	**did**	they	**do**?	They	**took**	surfing lessons.

Grammar Charts

Future "Be / Going to"

Yes / No Questions					Answers			
Be + subject + **going to** + *verb* ?					subject + *verb*			
Are	you	**going to**	*get*	*a good job?*	*Yes,*	I	*am.*	
Is	she	**going to**	*have*	*children?*	*No,*		she 's	not.
Are	they	**going to**	*be*	*rich?*	*No,*		they 're	not.

WH- Questions					Answers			
question word + *(be)* + subject + **going to** + *verb*?					Subject + *be* + **going to** + *verb*			
Where	**are**	they	**going to**	*live*?	They' **re**	**going to**	*live*	*in New Zealand.*
What	**is**	she	**going to**	*be*?	She' **s**	**going to**	*be*	*a teacher.*
What	**are**	you	**going to**	*do*?	I' **m**	**going to**	*learn*	*English.*

Future "Will"

Yes / No Questions				Short Answers			
Will + subject + *verb* …?				subject + **will / won't**			
Will	they	*be*	*famous?*	*Yes,*	I	**will**.	
Will	he	*work*	*hard?*	*No,*	she	**won't**.	
Will	you	*win*	*a prize?*	*Yes,*	they	**will**.	

WH- Questions				Answers			
question word + **will** + subject + *verb*?				Subject + **will** + *verb*			
Where	**will**	they	*live*?	They' **ll**	*live*	*in the U.S.*	
What	**will**	he	*win*?	He' **ll**	*win*	*a new car.*	
What	**will**	you	*do*?	I' **ll**	*get*	*a good job.*	

Grammar Charts

Common Irregular Verbs

Base Form	Past Simple
be	was, were
begin	began
bring	brought
buy	bought
choose	chose
come	came
do	did
drink	drank
eat	ate
feel	felt
get	got
give	gave
go	went
have	had
hear	heard
know	knew
leave	left
make	made
meet	met
read	read
ride	rode
say	said
see	saw
send	sent
sleep	slept
spend	spent
take	took
tell	told
think	thought
write	wrote